Seventeen and

SEVENTEEN &

Lovely to meet you.

We will never know, Patrick.

To all who have ever been, who wish to be, who try somehow to forget.

I wish you the most well being day, month, year of your life always.

Best wishes for Everything

Aidan McNally

17 & Life.

STAGES.

Confusion all around.

Alcohol Hello..

Hindsight.

School days.

Seventeen & Embarrassed.

What about cops.

What is "Honest" ?

The Cops.

School is Great.

How Silly.

DRINIING ALCOHOL.

Drug of choice.

What are emotions?

Scouts

Decision times

Memories Too

MAKE a CHOICE, TAKE a STAND

Good people.

Quiet Morning.

Positive Upswing.

The DOOR opens.

CONFUSION ALL AROUND

Sleep is just not going to happen. Some of the stuff these guys are shouting at each other, to give you an idea. "You are a dead man tomorrow, don't dare step out of your cell, I will be waiting" sounds oh so nice doesn't it ? Another is arguing about what he is owed and shouting more threats, it is almost like they are picking on certain people who are just not answering back or something. They yell even louder to get an answer. I am beginning to feel a little for whomever is the subject of theses threats.

It is like as if there are a few unsettled issues going on, every so often a new voice comes out and says something like, "shut up you had your chance and you are mouth, you will do nothing" they know this voice though because there is no aggression back to this person. It as if they know him to be a boss like or a dominant one. The accent of Dublin Ireland, I should try and take a little time to explain, it is known as a harsh and strong accent among the people of Dublin. The real inner city accent has a touch to it that is automatically detected as threatening and fierce and so these guys shouting are pretending to be tough by using a harsher accent, they are true dubs and naturally hard. Well I suppose when you take a look around where I now find myself, a prison cell, why would it surprise me that these guys are the real deal and the real criminals of the city. I am stuck in amongst them.

My own hangover has been starting to kick in and some feelings of weakness, physical weakness are tingling up and down and around my body. I am sitting on the edge of my bed now, or is it better called a bunk? A cot perhaps, a military type cot that is as basic a single bed as you can imagine. I sit up here listening to noises from the cell block, the white of the fluorescent lights from under my door and I have my head in my hands. There is light from a moon coming through my lovely plexiglass window, not much mind you but I am staring at nothing. I am noticing everything but I am definitely finding it hard to concentrate.

Having a headache coming on and the feeling of my head being too heavy in my own hands. I have a bump or two around my scull too, the one on the right hand side of my head I have touched it a couple of times by mistake, with my finger as I cradled my head in my hands, I tell you honestly it is beginning to feel a little more sore now as the hangover is getting stronger. Tipping the wound on my head by accident just isn't a smart thing and so I have been tipping gently trying to investigate exactly how bad is it. For me it is feeling like a gaping hole in my head, ah it's probably not that bad is all I can think about it for now as there is no getting a couple of aspirin at this hour in this place.

Prison, ya know? I do not think they make bedside visits with medication and are not too worried as to my well being. I am a criminal to them and so deserve less I guess.

Some of the guys shouting are definitely bullying, one guy is crying out for his mother and he is genuinely crying, all the others seem to get excited by this and the cell block comes to life with both bullies and some genuine guys shouting words of encouragement. "Go on and kill yourself, you will never survive tomorrow when we get our hands on you" like who even thinks that could be funny? The more genuine guys are shouting encouragement "don't worry a sentence goes by fast and you can do it on your back" on your back means you can do it lying down and the sentence will be easy like taking a nap. It will be over before you know it, so "on your back" is the term that people use.

I cannot say I am too proud of myself to know such use of words that are flying back and forth amongst the prisoners but I have not been keeping the best of company or friends lately and these are the kind of things I have learned. I never imagined I would need to know these kinds of interpretations but hey everything comes to us for a reason I suppose. A night in jail with full blown hangover and the worst yelling and screaming and now the moaning from guys outside on the cell block. I do not even have a clue what time it is at the moment, the moon of course helping me out to know we are well into the night but exact time I have no idea. The prison officers are walking up and down on the different levels and every so often there is a bang, a loud knock of the prisoner officer banging the door of the louder ones telling them to shut up. If they don't they will be put on report is the threat the officers call out to the inmates who keep mouthing off. Now on report I am not too sure of but it quiets them for like five minutes.

The sky outside the window is a black night of course but there is a blue hue to it all, is this my hangover or is it the cold? Hard to know but the city night is going on out there. Here and there I hear a truck engine revving and driving off into the distance, maybe taking off from a stop at a red light or something. What it does let me know though is there is not much traffic out there on the streets so we must be ten or eleven o clock I am thinking. Man there is nothing worse than a full hangover, the body aches and the head aches and even hearing your own pulse in you ears is almost too much noise. The bones in my body feel so weak, I know they are not weak or about to break or anything but it is a weakness that is maybe more like feeling frail or something. 17 years old and I feel like an old man who looks like his bones might break at any time for no reason, that is my feeling. My hands are sore, even holding my jaw up in the palm of my hand is causing it's own new pains too. Jesus Christ what on earth is coming over me and if these clowns outside could just shut up for a little while I might be able to think a little more.

I need to get back on track and get back to piecing this whole mess together. The pain in my head, the gaping hole on the side of my head is getting worse all the time, what on earth did I hit my head off last night like seriously this is no joke at all.

Seventeen and Life

What new world awaits me tomorrow, what criminals am I going to have to face and will I have to fight my way through the next few days, like yeah physically fight people to get some peace? It is my first time in here in jail so I have no clue what's ahead. Even when the prison officer was processing me in earlier, what a fool I was. Me 6 feet tall and a little bit extra all full of tough man attitude and the prison officer takes me to get out of my civilian clothes and change into the prison clothes, he instructs me to place my jacket on the floor, lay it down how he says, lay it out on the floor. He instructs me to put my shoes in the shoulder areas of my jacket, one in each corner of where the arms are. Me the bloody fool trying not to get in any trouble at all with the prison officer, I stand legs apart with one shoe in the shoulder area and the other in the other just as he had instructed me. Are you stupid? He asks me, take the shoes off and place them inside of the jacket. Was I the fool or what? I can only say it was my nerves and the overall feeling of how I am so out of my element now, no smart talking my way out of this one now that I am in the prison and there is no getting out. Innocence again, trying to be obliging to the man in power now but not thinking straight at all with the whole new desperation feeling of being locked up. What a fool alright.

There is a lull in the roaring and I can hear very little, must be folks are starting to fall asleep or something, I can peek out through the spy hole on my door and see the whole cell block of across the landing. The doors are a light green colour and they appear to be all tiny cause of the concave view I have. Steel walkways along the front of the doors and a big open area from my side across to the others. It seems like I am on a corner or something or the view angle of the spy hole but it is as if I can see my immediate neighbour as well as directly across from me. As I watch out I can see guys swinging a line from out the corner of their own door, they seem to passing joints or cigarettes. The guy doing it reels it back in and sends it out again with a swing as it goes to his neighbour, the neighbour has his own string with something weighted on the end of it to swing it and land across the line. He grabs it by help of the weighted end and reels the joint in to himself. I will have to admit to you that this seems real inventive, the prisons officers do not appear to be around or watching, I can hear them pacing but I cannot see them anywhere. This makes sense to me why those guys across the landing are taking their chance, they must know the whereabouts of the officer by the sound so to know they can get away with passing the contraband between each other, pretty smart is what I thought alright, pretty smart indeed.

With it being Sumner time now I can hear people from outside, the distant laughs and giggles of people chatting and it sounds to me like a crowd from a bar or a night club that have brought their good cheer out in to the street. It is hard to tell how close they are, distant yes but close enough to hear the chat yet not close enough to hear the precise words. The atmosphere type sound, my first thoughts, yup I wish I was among them right now, having a few pints of beer just to take away the horrible hangover. Sounds awesome to hear the fun of a bar, I sit back down on my bed and lay back to try to sleep, wishing away the pain in my head. This is the first time I have laid down on the bed, I lie back as if I am fully accepting of my new home. Weird how a bit of a hangover and the dreaming of being out among the crowd at the bar have put me at such ease. There is still some shouting out on the landing but way less now, the pub crowd take me all the way back to thinking of where did I get this thirst for the booze? When did I start thinking to be drinking alcohol was a great idea for me as a teenager?

ALCOHOL HELLO

Seventeen and Life

When I was small I used to sip the remains of the beer we would leave out for Santa Claus. If there was any drinking going on late at night in my home by my dad and his friends, it was rare but on occasion there would be a few glasses left on the kitchen table and when I would get up, on those mornings I would sip on the remains in the glasses.

Things did kick off more seriously for me when I was eleven or so, possibly twelve. I had an opportunity to venture off for a three week summer camp during the summer holidays from school. The camp is known as Gaeltacht, to clarify what exactly is gael-teacht it means in direct translation from the Irish language into English means "Irish house". Gael is the Irish language, known as gaeilge (Gale GA) and teacht (chock ~ed) in the Irish language means house so it is really easy and makes sense, doesn't it ? Didn't think so either.

The rules of the Gaeltacht are that students attending for the Sumner will not speak any English for their stay there and the three weeks there will be spent doing classes in the Irish language along with sporting in the afternoons where only Irish can be spoken and again in the evenings, which were entertainment evenings.

These entertainment evenings were awesome, sometimes it would be just Irish music on a player that would play set music sets to where we practiced and had teachers teaching us the Irish dance known as Ceili, pronounced KAY-LEE. This would consist of us being paired with a partner and of course this meant girls but we will get to that soon enough. So pair opposite pair and then we dance in and out from each other then we exchange partner and dance around and around and return to our position while our partners did the same, all the while we would keep time with our steps or clapping.

On other evenings live music would be played by visiting musicians who, played the Irish instruments to the same type, "set dance" of Irish ceili music.

The Gaeltacht had a routine every day and evening and we were housed in a family home or host family, these families spoke exclusively Irish in their household and we stayed with them. Breakfast was prepared for us and we would head off to school for 9 am. The children in the house found it funny that we didn't know any Irish, they would ask us questions and my own basic Irish would try and answer back but they knew Irish as their first language and for me from Dublin who only had what I had learned in national school as a child.

We would take Irish classes in the morning and then head back home for our lunch, returning to school for more Irish classes and then some sporting activity for the afternoon. All the time the only requirement on us children was to speak only our native tongue the Irish language, Gaeilge. We would then head home to our host family and our dinner was served to us. I shared a room with two other guys and there were two other guys across the hall from us. There was one other younger guy, not as young as me mind you and then three other older guys, they had explained to me that they were mature students in college or university and Irish was a key part to them passing their college year, so really they were there to learn and they did take more intense classes during the day. After dinner was shower time and head back to the school for our night of entertainment.

The girls would be dressed up and always were looking well, it was a requirement to dance with a partner, so the first order of business was asking a girl to dance and then she would be your partner for the evening. I had my eye on some of the girls during the day in class and sometimes in the sports we were paired as partners boy and girl so I was getting to know some of them. Also during practice ceili nights we did have the chance to switch and mix partners through the different set dances. At the dance night there was always the hype that maybe there could be some kissing done so it was all to play for on ceili night.

Seventeen and Life

Being that I was twelve I was for sure one of the younger boys on the summer camp. Although I was big for my age and always taken to be a bit older, I was able to blend in and most of the other children on the summer trip to the Gaeltacht were around sixteen or so, some fourteen or fifteen and the odd seventeen or eighteen year old but the majority being around sixteen. I had all these strangers in front of me everyday and every evening and yes the girls were good looking. All the boys were zoning in on some of the absolutely gorgeous ones that were there. I remember I used to play tennis with this one girl who enjoyed a good game, I was pretty handy at tennis and we spent some sunny afternoons playing on the courts to the back of the school, she was one of the hottest girls and all the boys wanted to date her, some would even hang out by the tennis court while we played. She was an older girl seventeen and a beautiful girl, I started seeing her as my friend and tennis partner and we shared some laughs, even about how she hates all these guys drooling over her. We shared tennis courts and dances in the evenings and though we were not doing any kind of boyfriend or girlfriend type of thing some of the other guys sure did give me a hard time about it when she was not around. I wanted to shift her for sure, "shift" was our simple term for kissing back then, but I had no pressing need to have to kiss her. I was still too young and innocent to be preoccupied with this kind of thing yet, that innocence in tact at the eleven / twelve mark.

The Gaeltacht areas of Ireland are dotted around the four corners of the country and are differing in dialect or pronunciation of the same language, Irish of course. The small villages where the Gaeltachts are, are rural and do not have any big town names associated with them. Our little village had two little shops and a petrol station, further up the road a church not too far from the school we attended. The

Seventeen and Life

houses where we stayed were dotted around the western part of Ireland which is known as Connemara, it is the western part of Ireland west from the larger city of Galway. The homes dotted around the landscape of rugged rock and some big open type landscape. In the shop of the village we were only allowed to speak Irish and there was one boy who had been reported to be sent home because he was caught speaking English in the shop, the shop keeper had reported him to the school and there was no forgiving this. He had broken the rules and was sent home.

The older boys staying in the same house as me were more serious about their classes and their learning but they did not worry too much about speaking English everywhere else. They were mature students and most of their nights were spent in the local pub after school hours. They would come home for dinner sometimes a little drunk and then go to the school dance and even leave early from the dance to go back to the pub. Seeing as this was my first real freedom summer and the being away from home, alone and really enjoying myself. I had been away from home before on some cub scout camps when I was eight and nine and ten but this was different. I was now away by myself with all brand new faces, with the cub scouts I had known everybody for some years and we were all really growing up together from around the local town. The gaelteacht was giving me the opportunity to be an individual and really enjoy it all, new friends. The school was fun and I was learning the Irish language well and one of the best looking girls on the camp was giving me all the perfect signs of being interested in me, she was spending lots of time with me and we did kind of fool around a little on the beach on the way home from school already. The guys in my house had bought some cans of beer from the pub and had them in the house, after dinner one evening and prior to showering and heading for the dance, they shared their cans with me. This was great, they gave me two cans and we drank in the room, I loved the hanging out and drinking beer, how amazing was this. A nice dizzy drink with the real smell of older man off my breath. A couple of cans of beer that set my mind a buzzing. I have heard people call getting drunk getting a "heat on" and I was for sure in the west of Ireland getting a heat on in my little twelve year old body. It was almost just assumed that I was around sixteen so nobody saw anything weird by offering me a few cans of the hard stuff.

I went to the ceili that one night and felt like I was so buzzing I had a confidence that was something completely new, a new stride I walked with, to be on top of the world, drunk with a whole new language I was speaking and the beautiful girl to dance with. Who could not want any of this magic all at once, the magic of being young and free along with thinking and speaking Irish like a native of the gaelteacht area and after the dance kissing my new girl, I remember her pulling back from me and spitting out the taste of the beer and she didn't like the taste at all, she was very clear we were going back into the dance and she handed me two sticks of chewing gum saying we could come back out in a while once I had chewed on these for a while.

My new love, and how fine and sweet a love it was that I had found in the west of Ireland, all those miles from home and free. Free to kiss girls and smoke when ever I wanted and the best looking girls too, I might add, yes I know, you might have thought of my lovely new girlfriend as being my new love but no, I had found my taste for drinking alcohol. Cans of beer were beautiful. That summer when I was in the gaelteacht was quite a hot summer and the older boys now always had a tray of beer in the house so I could give them some money and get four cans, one of them had a car and one time we went to the local city for a spin and he took my

Seventeen and Life

money and bought me my own stash of cans. The buzz of being drunk was awesome and what was not to like, did I know then that throughout innocence of thinking I was cool, I mean come on right? I had the girl, no parents to reprimand me and everything going absolutely wonderful. How could anyone not think this new stuff was great?

I do not recall any peer pressure at all, these guys were quite my senior so I viewed them as adults really, not my peers. I just took a chance at it and I liked drinking, everything seemed to, well it just seemed to work right for me. How could I think there was any wrong in being so young and so wrong for drinking. I did not think that way at all, there is the innocence of youth for sure. Oh please do not get me wrong about the gaelteacht, this is a real coming of age kind of experience for a young teenager, perhaps I was a little too young. But learning Irish and being fully immersed in Irish everywhere was amazing, at home with the host family and in the school by day and by night, in the local shop and even if when you were walking to or from school should you might meet someone from the area walking along the road, they would greet you in Irish too. If anyone ever wants to learn the Irish language or Irish dance. Head to Connemara and find a gaelteacht to attend or even look up some ceili dances as they will teach you the steps, even on any dance night, how to step to beautiful Irish music.

That summer brought me to my new found passion and an appreciation for the taste of beer. Cans of beer and me had now become real good buddies after that. I learned to speak fluent Irish too, but the one item that had begun from that summer, well let's just say, we unleashed the lion that year in the gaelteacht.

Was I too young, yes absolutely but did I like it?, you better believe it. What lesson was there, I am trying to recall, being too young as I said that is for certain, freedom may always not be the best for a young boy who thinks he can be a man. That is the word alright, the word of this night, the word that is bouncing around in my subconscious and clattering off the walls of my brain it seems that way from the pounding headache getting worse. Freedom, look at how tonight in my prison cell that freedom has now just shot up in value, freedom? I have abused it and they have decided to take it away from me. Seventeen years of age and have been abusing my freedom for the past five years and a piece but not quite a full six years.

"Value your freedom" has never rung through to me so clearly, can it be the freezing cold of this cell or maybe the reality of where I am sitting that it takes this kind of shock to the system to see clear of what the things we have taken for granted and in my case even abused, my freedom now gone. Or is it just that a serious hangover brings about some guilt and a harsher look at things? No matter which and however someone might want to view or value what their freedom means to them (you) I can tell you out straight, sitting in a prison cell is a tiny, just a tad bit late for having the realizations about freedom.

I can see now as an adult, of course that being a child was a very innocent time in life and reflecting back to when I was seventeen is much easier as the power of hind sight and all the very clear vision we are afforded when looking back with an older head of wisdom, is that, don't you remember being young? Being a teenager who really said to themselves everyday, I don't care ! Well I did not care, look where it landed me. But again as I am now in my forties I can say with all great confidence, I did not just speak my words as a teenager, nope I lived them. The beauty of knowing now is of course a terrible set of ironic cards to have to be dealt, when recalling all the messed up days but getting lost in the memories of pure and innocent play and thoughts that ran through my brain back then.

Seventeen and Life

The innocence was going away fast and after that gaelteacht summer, I had advanced to continuing to drink alcohol but now much more on a regular basis. I would find a way to earn some money so I could buy cans of beer.

With a new found social life and socializing with kids who are drinking, what is there not to like for any the young boy "man" about hanging out with girls. Of course it is new and unusual to be "making out" or "getting off" with girls as it is a whole new world to me. Kissing is one thing but this idea that I had, that a girl wants to feel good when she is with you and she will for sure be telling her friends, well it is important to perform to the best of my ability isn't it?

In these young teenage years are we perfecting our flirt or have we had it since we were a toddler? When the grown ups used to do the goo and the gaa at us sitting motionless in our buggy. Did we begin at that young age perfecting our flirt game. Well at thirteen years of age it has become important why we might just need this animalistic ritual of puffing out our plumage to attract the opposite sex to begin an adventure, at first I thought being a great kisser was very important. My mind said to me, be a good kisser and you will be able to kiss all night if you want and possibly not only one girl, many more if they hear you are a good kisser then they might want some of it too. How could I know any different about that. When I was even younger I can remember doing the kissing game after school which was so dumb, now thinking back, we advanced quickly from the peck on the lips to "French kissing" little bags of testosterone that is for sure what we were. Girls feel soft and nice and are for sure a pleasure to kiss, who can deny this?

But with this new social scene there is the whole aspect of kissing and holding their breasts and rubbing them and feeling the woman element of their being, nice! yes absolutely. I would get a little drunk and off I go to try and "shift" a girl, I had like I said some experiences already and not only was I enjoying their bodies but I also wanted them to enjoy mine. It is just like all the movies of any young boy becoming teenager, yes you guessed it, when is she going to hold my, you know what.

I can remember a night at a party, sounds so grown up to say party, some other kids had a house all to themselves and so all of us kids found our way there and we could do our drinking in the house and all hang out together. We were all in the bedroom for some strange reason and the lights had been turned off. The beds were bunk beds so we were in the children's room of the house, three guys and three girls, I was kissing this girl in the top bunk and she had let me, well because it was important to me that she was okay with me fooling around with her boobs and that I was being allowed to fondle her as we kissed. I wanted to press myself against her so she could feel how hard I was getting. She had awesome hair this girl and while I was kissing her, she was kissing me back good and hard too. I remember feeling her hair sometimes with my other hand and she was arching her back as if to get comfortable in the little top bunk bed, but also forcing her breast harder into my hand. I was laying to her side and across her one leg and making sure she could feel that my newly awakened penis was pressing hard upon her. What are we doing are the thoughts in a young guys mind at those exact moments, yes indeed they are, how do I get her to touch it? Voluntarily of course, how can it be that she will just slide her hand down my pants and rub me some?

These are high energy thoughts that flow through a mind that is already in an overdrive status, what with concentrating on keeping the tongue wrestling going and plenty of lip nibbling to a steady motion of hands on nipples and a hard on being pressed into her gently, in the absolute no way forceful as possible without her jumping up running out and calling me a rapist or something weird. The dilemma a young teenager has at those precise moments are quite the juggling act. Yes I know we all have had our first experiences and each a little different but I say with hi confidence that the majority of us guys thought a million miles a second that "if she will just touch it, it will be brilliant" of course when she did, it had to be the most amazing experience ever. And she did not embarrass me or let anyone else know what was going on. We were making out for real now, I could not concentrate on anything anymore, her breasts were awesome and nipples like cigar butts firm and thick, thick.

How can anyone not think that going out on a weekend and having a few drinks along with some kissing and some, well almost sex, how could anyone fault this new social life and lifestyle?

Oh yeah being twelve going on thirteen was just not the right time for this, perhaps. Of course I am forgetting that all the other kids are sixteen and seventeen, they were having sex for real now and I am just figuring all this out for the first time. Like I said, how could this be faulted? Some of my friends and classmates were probably, looking back at it now, they were developing away at a "normal" rate or pace and I was out there going as fast as I could.

What is a kid to actually know about any of it, sex is what I am talking about, of course. Like for example of how much I actually knew, they did some tiny little one day of a brush over the subject in school when we were about twelve. Some introductory standard stuff, telling us about reproductive organs and how fertilization occurs. How the male parts produce the sperm and of course the female produces the egg, whoop de doo ! On that subject.

Where the hell is the education about turning the girl on and getting her super horny or what about tell us what joy it is to "politely" force her hand or her head onto my manliness. What about her even? What is a good time to go for it and start getting involved in her? Like will her kiss let me know it

Seventeen and Life

is okay to start touching her and feeling her up? These are all very important issues a young teenage boy needs to know. Like I was mentioning earlier, a young boy like me wanted to kiss and "swap spit" French kiss and of course when my dick is getting harder and harder, I want her to know about it. Not only so she can be aware and here comes the tricky part, the pressure we feel. I want her to take an interest in it, I want her to just know what to do with an erection, I certainly and most definitely do not want her freaking out and going to tell her friends and end up the joke of the evening for her friend's giggles, just cause I am a boy who wants some action. But for another example I recall many situations where I was so hard with an erection I would be doing my best kissing and of course hand motions for her titties, maybe even suckling her nipples and wanted nothing more for her to take over but never knew how to ask, like seriously where was that in sex education day? So what else is there to do except start to guide her hand slowly and cunningly really, to the erection.

We fellas get just exactly that, cunning, when it comes to getting a girl to touch that bursting erection. As a teenager I have never knew exactly what the real pleasure of sex even was, but I was always bursting to find out.

Ireland is full of good girls as in the years of my being teenager, by default being Irish meant being Catholic school girls and of course if any of the playboy articles I had ever read meant, I was fooling around and had every chance of being with the best girls for great sex. So with all this in ones mind right at the time of "spit swapping" how on earth can a boy stay focused. Make her feel like, you know what you are doing but more importantly make it so she is certain you know how, no time for getting laughed at. I wanted to be sexual and I wanted it returned but I could have used some help in figuring that out, thanks a bunch, Irish sex education for nothing, do you really think I am thinking about sperm fertilizing eggs and tubes and wombs when all I need is some dick attention, you guessed it, furthest from my mind and I will go out on a limb and say, no other young fella wants to know about it either. The whole time is spent focussing on how in the hell can I get her touching it and caressing it.

That's the ultimate goal of the whole process.

There is nothing too fancy or complicated in any of this making out business. I did want some kissing too and it feels great to have a girl just touching me in any way really.

I had a girl that wanted to be my girlfriend and she was older than me by a few years, I was thirteen and she was seventeen. I remember her turning eighteen, anyway, she would do all the kissing and cuddling and make me feel very relaxed. She had a massive pair of boobs and her tongue was velvet soft, always a fresh minty breath and when she put her hands on me I loved it. She broke it off with me and I didn't understand why. We had fooled around but I never crossed the line or tried to get the all clear from her and I just couldn't bring myself to force the situation and she never gave me any of the "all clear" signals. Her friend who was a guy told me that she had confided in him that I didn't fuck her and she wanted it so bad. Now how on earth was I supposed to know this? I didn't know and felt like a clown. All that time with me trying to be respectful and the tons of evenings we spent "dry humping" and all she wanted was the same thing as me. Being young and everybody thinking I was older had it's hard moments, pressure to perform and I had not a clue of what "perform" even meant in that context. Yet somehow I was instinctively horny as hell and wanted all the "perform" I could get. I think she lied to her friends and told them stories that we had done it a few times cause once she let me go and we were no longer boyfriend and girlfriend, well now the fun started.

We were out drinking one evening, a big group of us and it was normal to be hiding away from the cops and getting drunk. A bunch of teenagers doing no harm to anyone but ourselves. Well this particular night, my ex girlfriend had one

Seventeen and Life

of her friends there and some how we were walking off together for a chat. A chat and some alone time, we left the crowd behind us and headed towards the beach were we could hang out together of course and "chat". I was still just that young boy who had no clue about any of this sex business and she thinks I am seventeen or eighteen, I am down for the kissing or shifting or "getting off with" as we used to call it. The kissing started to get a little hot and heavy on the beach and she had no problem taking hold of me firmly, she was actually tugging on me a little hard even and I was not sure what was going on exactly. I must have been panicking or something because I convinced her that the sand was too uncomfortable and we decided to head back to where she was staying. She was spending the night at her friends house, her and the girls doing a sleep over. As we got closer to the house she told me that there was no way she could get me into the house cause it's girls only and the parents are home too. All she, well they needed to do was not be caught being drunk but boys no way!

As we walked up the street closer to her friend's house, we were hugging and stopping along the way for some kissing but now I was back to wishing to be touched, it wasn't happening like at the beach, screwed it up for myself and anticipation was where I was left. We stopped just down the street from the house and started kissing again, she kept saying "I wish I could bring you in for the night but it is impossible, I can stay out for a while though" so we got to making out some more and now this time she took a hold of me again, oh yeah!!! Now we are getting down to business, we lay on the grass and with me fooling around with her and she was wet, really wet and I was really hard. My dick sliding inside of her pussy, it was happening, kissing and nipple play, nibbling sometimes and her holding on to my ass helping me stride back and forth. This is sex, we are doing it, this feels amazing. My head had gone into a spin now by this stage, to feel her tongue move from mouth to my ear and whispering to me how she knew I was good, don't stop, don't stop she kept on saying. I was unsure how long this had been going on, like for real I had forgotten everything and in a moment amidst the throws of young teenage passion I felt like I was eight feet tall and very hulk like, unstoppable. She started groaning a little and I was so concerned that I might be hurting her I slowed to ask, she said "no no, please! Don't stop" my thoughts jumped back to pay attention to what I was doing, then the young dumb element kicked in. My mind starts freaking out again, questions in my head popping off like fireworks, "how long has it been? " everyone says it won't last long if you are "no good" concentrate, concentrate man was how my mind was trying to keep me focused and to be honest this had been a goal of mine for a while now and the fact it's actually happening, do not mess it up. "You better last a long time, focus on her, make her enjoy this too" the words from a brand new voice in my mind, my sexual control voice that just seemed to appear, in an, all of a hurry kind of way.

And thank you very much for the sex education because sperm and eggs did not enter my mind at all, "better stop or she will get pregnant" is on one half of my mind which I suppose is conscience, the other half which must be the little devil we all have on our shoulders, well he is winning "This is sex and this is awesome, keep going feel how she feels wet all over your dick, this is what you crave"

Somewhere in the middle of all the tongue wrestling and her whispering to me and my mind not able to think straight, not even for a second, everything is spinning and we are fucking, having sex or making love. This reality was becoming a little overwhelming and then I can feel from the very base of my balls a tingling, an awesome tingling. Not only from her rubbing them with her hand but something real new, she pulled me in closer and I pulled back out something was a

Seventeen and Life

stirring, legs beginning to shake almost, I pulled my dick out from her and spewed hot cum everywhere. I knew the only thing I would be fertilizing would be the grass beneath us, or a few little weeds. We kissed a little more and I headed home, she went off in to the girls night at her friend's house and me, I was walking the roadway home with all the prancing of the proud stallion that I had now become.

That summer there were a few more girls who wanted some of the action and who was I to refuse. Was this my summer of love? Love making, for sure.

I remember the phone call the following day, her friends pretending to be her, trying to talk like her and catch me out by saying "oh I am so sore" and other silly things. I knew it was them and they were giggling, saying they saw her chest and it was really red so somebody was doing a lot to her chest. I denied all and did not really realize the other girls were trying to get some too.

Seventeen and Life

Oh yes it was a nice summer.

Looking back at it now and even though the whole new sex thing was great. And feeling my way around a girls body, learning what to do and how to do it even better made for some great times and I think back and often wonder, why did that come so easy too. Maybe if it were a little more difficult to get laid perhaps it would have been a calming effect over me. A little struggle involved, something difficult, not just being able to talk my way into a girls panties.

Look at me now, sitting in a prison cell for the very reason of things just had to come to me just too easy. All has just always been too easy. Nothing would have been wrong with a challenge or two. I wanted to do everything, the girls and the drugs, the fights in the streets and do whatever I chose to do. No adults telling me what to do, just me and my mind ruling my life and no adults to dictate to me.

Seventeen and Life

This cell of mine is getting colder and it must be the wee hours of the morning. It is getting colder, of course the open air window doesn't help. The screaming and yelling has quietened down a little but not totally. I still ache and need to focus for my first day in the general population. Make a game plan, stick to it, focus on survival. It is my first time in prison so I better have my A game. Why I cannot sleep? Nerves, perhaps. Of course the come down from last night's escapade of booze and dope, that's what landed me here in the first place.

Ah fuck it, a little sleep, come on head, just calm down a while. Give me some shot of a few hours kip. Let me sleep it off for a while. Looking at the walls and the carvings of those that have been here before me. There is plenty of scratchings just like in the movies. You know the ones that somebody was counting their days, four vertical lines with the fifth line scratched across at a diagonal. Other names carved into the plaster of the walls, Damo & Johno are easy to make out.

One of them the name is faded, could say Paullie or might even say Patsy, hard to make out but they were here in '88 who ever they are. The wall is like an old cottage wall, large stone's held together by plaster of some old sort of adobe looking type mixture. Bottom line these are old walls for sure. The carvings are in the roof too, looks like an old concrete slab, with the signs of boredom from the previous occupants.

The choices in life that have lead me here, the decisions to go left when maybe I should have went right. The chances I had to have a girlfriend but thought it always better to be free and single, play the field as they used to say. So many things can run through your mind just laying here all deflated. My bones even feel weak. There has always been choices to make and by the look of my surroundings the decisions have been poor ones. It really is amazing what power of thought and a decision has in our life, the simplest way of thinking can affect so much. I always thought I never did any harm, the authorities apparently think differently.

Of course it is easier to reflect back now that I am older, being older does not give to any great automatic qualification to wisdom. The bit it does help is getting the benefit of hind sight. Being older let's your mind think just a little more, your joints and muscles ache differently and more often.

Hindsight, how great it is. Reflecting back sitting in a prison cell and thinking about what went wrong?, only now 17 years of age and the brakes have been put on. Taking stock of all the memories and trying to think even more, I didn't even think it was possible to think some more. Re-evaluating life at only 17, seems a bit much for a young person, a whole life ahead and already thinking back about it, seems a little early in my years or early in life to be thinking back doesn't it?

Seventeen and Life

Why would anyone have to think back some and look at their life at all? Some screwed up situation has to happen for us in order for any of us to look back and piece together what did happen. I did not care too much about anything ever really. Not a care about who or what or even when. Yet a situation like sitting here in a prison cell, well that can make a whole pile of difference, all the memories come flooding back and all at once too.

Why is that ?

Seventeen and Life

We humans are funny creatures if we really would like to dissect how the whole brain and thinking process goes. What do we actually know, about ourselves?

At what age do we begin to know who we really are and more so at what point in any of this, at what point do we question all of our make up?

At 17 years of age, sitting on an uncomfortable mattress, I found myself thinking about precisely this. Although being totally honest, I never asked myself, who have I become? I wanted to know more things along the lines of, how did I get caught or has it all come to an end, will I ever get out of here or the deepest would definitely have to be, why am I here? Something somewhere went amiss. I did not concern myself too much that I was in prison, well not totally, like yes sure I wash more stomped or astonished at the fact some prison guard was passing by outside and peering in at me through the little spy hole in my cell door. This now had become my window to the outside world. The "shock and awe" of my new prison home, yes this definitely brought me to the conversation with myself of, WTF !!!

It is for sure a moment like this in life that I can vividly remember beginning to think about, who am I? Just not to any super depth though. I guess just deep enough at that time, given the bursting hangover and the noisy new neighbours I have found myself amongst.

HINDSIGHT

It is amazing how we can look back over things we have done in our life, when we sum it all up it is like well, not even a ten minute clip from a film/movie.

Incidents and accidents says one old classic song, seriously though, taking stock of events in our past. I wonder is it that we remember the early items because it was the first time? Like our first time experience of something or is it a vivid memory because it was the very first time we felt a certain way? I can hazard a guess that it is the feeling we remember, the first time we felt something happen for us.

The thing that makes us remember so well is the point inside of us that remembers, we might forget the actual colour of our clothes that particular day or the person we met in the newsagents shop that morning, what did they say in passing that morning? But we can remember the experience we had at our first this or first that because the feeling, the new same feeling was real and intense and new. This helps us to remember, that is what I believe at least. It is our inner self piece that clearly remembers how we felt or a certain feeling that we felt for our very first time, ever.

I remember the first time I got absolutely, shit faced drunk. Not the first time I got drunk, the first time I got hammered, twisted drunk and of course this is the part where I let you in on that piece of the little terror I was as a young fella.

It is a vivid memory because of how I felt, I decided to make a raid on the drinks cabinet at home. I was round about 11 years old that year, It was early summer and I remember a nice sunny day and for some funny reason I decided it would be a great idea to rob some alcohol from the drinks cabinet and see what all these spirits were all about?

I had a two litre plastic bottles, it was one of the ones orange squash came in, a kind of dilute with water to taste thing. Empty of course, I didn't want any diluting going on with my alcohol this particular day. The drinks cabinet at home was not locked or anything and why should it be? There were no reasons for it to be locked, so I started pouring out bottles of foul smelling alcohol into my plastic bottle. I tried not to take too much of any one drink so as not to leave anything too noticeable for my mother or father to catch on too quickly. A little of some of the clear liquids, well a little more of those cause I could fill them back up with water and it couldn't be noticed. Knowing what I know now about alcohol, I will say they were, gin, vodka and some poitin. What is poitin? Well it is the moonshine hooch of Ireland, illegal they say but everyone seemed to have a bottle of the stuff somewhere in their house.

On to the darker bottles, again a few drops here and there, some whiskey and then some more whiskey as there were three different bottles of whiskey in the cabinet. I had this liquorice smelling drink which I cannot recall the name of and a few other liquors of some sort or other. I had myself a 2 litre concoction of liquids that quite seriously may even have been explosive for all that I knew. The drinks cabinet was always kind of full of stuff as I remember my Mam & Dad doing some entertaining from time to time, business partners of my Dad's or some of his clients. I remember falling asleep as a child to the sound of their laughter coming from the sitting room in our house. The only time there was beer there was at Christmas time cause me and my brother would have to leave a beer for Santa. Those Christmas mornings when I would rush to the sitting room, not to see what presents had been left for me under the tree, oh no! I wanted to check and see did Santa only drink half of his beer, which meant half for me on Christmas morning, of course.

How and ever, a bottle of toxic alcohol poison all filled up and ready to go. My friend and neighbour at the time was a year or so older than me and he had said to me how his parents were away for a few nights and he wanted to get drunk. The plan being we both do a raid for alcohol in our homes and meet up a little later on that afternoon, so that's exactly what we did. I may have been ten years old that year, I want to say I was eleven but there is a real chance I was only ten.

We met up together and my friend had gotten two cans of beer, large cans of harp larger and a mid size bottle of vodka and away we walked off up our road, all giddy of course and this buzz between us of how we are "gonna get buzzed and wasted tonight" where were we going? We really had no idea, we could not stay at my house as my mother and brothers were there and even though his parents were away his older cousin was doing the babysitting for them and no way would we get away with it there either. When we got to the top of our road we decided to head to our local town of Skerries. We had some options to head to a few different parts of the different beaches or an area known as the "ballast pit" which was an old empty pit in the ground with a section of it all overgrown with brambles and briars, nobody would see us there. We headed for the ballast pit and ended up taking up refuge in the shelter of the platform at the train station, a little waiting area with a roof and a bench. Ideal if anyone would approach us we could hide the drink inside our jackets and say we are waiting for the next train. The police would not get a jump on us as we were on the opposite side of the tracks from the entrance to the train station and so we had the perfect full view of the station, should any problems come our way to interfere with our plans we could get the head start on a getaway. We drank the beer along with sharing gulps of the mixture I had made for us. We were daring each other to take bigger gulps and laughing at the faces each other made, because trust me when I say this mix was poxy to the taste.

When all our alcohol was gone and with us continuing to try and convince each other we were not drunk yet we headed for the town, buckled is of course an understatement.

That summers evening was coming to a close though not quite dark yet, Ireland is funny that way in the summer months, it can stay bright until nearly midnight some nights and so to know the actual time of evening was almost impossible especially allowing for our condition of course but the street lights were starting to come on so it was somewhere between say 9 & 11pm roughly. I like the great genius that I am decided it would be funny to kick the base of the light poles as this was a way to make them go out again. I had seen it being done before and why not give it a go. I stumbled along the station road drunk out of my mind kicking each light pole as I passed it all along the way, my friend buckled in drunken laughter as each light went out. The more he laughed the harder I kicked the next one and so on. They only stay out for 15 or 20 minutes or so, so no real harm being done I figured.

On down the street we went and for some peculiar reason we took to a road into another housing estate area, to avoid the police seeing us as we could hardly stand up straight let alone walk straight. For some reason we ended up on a street that was a dead end, we did not know how to get out of there. All the houses on both sides of the street looked the same and there is a sweeping curve that leads down to the dead end of the street, this was the maze we were faced with. There were other kids out playing and they thought it hilarious to take my friend's jacket and laugh as he tried to chase them to get it

Seventeen and Life

back. These kids were not much younger than ourselves mind you. One of their mother's had come out and was asking for our names or she was calling the police. We gave some fake names and I pleaded with her to just show us the way out and we would be on our way, but no, this was not good enough for her. I had kept on saying to her "look lady, we are just really drunk and there is no need for police, tell us how to get out of this street and we are gone. We are just drunk" all the while my friend is falling on the pavement here there and everywhere. The woman went inside again with her threat of calling the police and we were basically screwed up every which way imaginable, what must she have thought really? She came back out calling us by our fake names, which seemed to be working and she agreed no need for police, just give her our mother's names and she will call them to come and pick us up. My friend now rolling around on the ground laughing stupidly at what seemed like nothing stuttered somewhere mid breath "me ma is away and she won't be able to answer" this he found to be the funniest thing ever although I laughed a bit too. So we continued with the lady and I asked her again, we just need to find our way back to Loughshinny, that is all we need.

Well we had used our classmates names and they are from Loughshinny too so no big problem there I thought. She went inside again and I went over to pick up my friend and as I was leaning over him and telling him that we need to get out of here, someone called out "Aidan", I stood up and answered yes and it was the woman. "Aidan Mc Nally, once you said Loughshinny I figured you out. I know your mother from the scouts committee and am calling her at once" Busted! Now I am leaning over my friend trying to get him to his feet and telling him what's going on and we need to get out of here real quick. It wasn't working though and he continued to roll around laughing.

My mother showed up in here car, little black mini car the long version. It was a mini clubman estate car to give it it's proper name, some of the lads called it the "Mc mobile" us being McNally and all, ya know little black car like the "bat mobile" anyway she pulled and dragged the two of us into the car. Off we went and she was driving a little bit mad I suppose, maybe she just had no idea what to do with us and was thinking about it all the way as we headed home where I was dragged to my feet again and into the house and left on the bathroom floor, my head propped over the toilet bowl as of course my puking vile alcohol spirits had began. My friend was taken down to his house but his parents were not there to receive him, lucky him.

I could hear my mother back in the house frantically going on and on about how she will have a full report for his mother when she returns. I cannot remember much more about that night? Other than the sore heaving and puking that seemed like it would never end. It was sore each and every time. A night of drinking at a very young age, what a disaster! Caught by my parents, embarrassed my mother and as they say in Ireland "made a holy show of the family" first time ever being caught drunk and first time ever being shit faced drunk, all in the one episode. I think I was grounded for like 20 years over that one, but as I so often did in my life, I didn't take the punishment too serious and I was back out and about before long.

Can alcohol really do all this? Land me in here, locked up! It sure seems like taking a trip down memory lane is what the whole first night in prison must have to be about, like what length of time am I going to have to spend here?

Talk about a screwed up situation now, I didn't even hear what the judge had to say properly, well he didn't even seem to concerned if I could understand him or not, yup, it's a screwed up situation alright, this is for sure. I should be writing a book for all to read about some of the fantastic

Seventeen and Life

things that I am going to do in my life, some of the dreams I have yet to fulfil, all the world that I want to travel and places to see. All my dreams of making good money and traveling, all taken away cause of my abuse of alcohol? They might lock up a young guy like me to teach me a lesson, maybe that's what all this first night in prison is all about. The trouble is that I may not have heard the judge properly but I am for sure certain if he had have mentioned anything about getting out well, I would have heard anything along those lines crystal clear.

There goes my little mouse again, the little fucker moves so fast and then stops almost in the same place every time, twitching his little nose or snout or whatever it's called. He is just right over there by the door sniffing away, almost has a look of disgust on his face. Is he the rep for the man above? Of who obviously is not in any way, shape or form in approval for what I have gone and done this time around. Or is he just a mouse that is none to fond of my large self taking over his stomping grounds? Who knows really, I have to figure that perhaps the last lad who lived in this shitty little 8x10 cell must have been feeding him or something, the little guy doesn't seem to be too bothered by me being human only that he keeps on twitching that nose. It is as if he knows the difference between us, he looks at me with a funny face, if I could put words to it, he is saying "look buddy, I choose to be here so be thankful for the company. You fucked up your life and ended up here, ya dumb ass! "

You know he is right, it is no matter to boast about, cops and courts and now held under lock and key. Seventeen years of age and locked up. There is no room for denying the reality of where I am or what I have become, all in only seventeen short years of life. An animal just like in the zoo or something, a person who cannot or did not value the freedom of life. The joy that is simple living, too young to understand that life has so much to offer. My choices and all of my decisions have been one bad one after another all leading me to this.

Now, where are the crossroads of life? I have come to many of them in my teenage years and did not recognize any of them, it seems that way now at least. This is the place for me, I do not belong here but there is nobody left that wants to hear that, at least not now. And if I know this to be the case, how then have I ended up here? The same question keeps coming back to me. Do I have an answer? Is there an answer or more seriously where did this problem all come from? What can a teenager know about life and all the joys and wonder that actually exist in everyday life, think about it, can you remember being 14 years old? Did you have the weight of the world on your shoulders to where you knew that each and every decision made would be the shaping of your future? I didn't get any lectures from anybody at 13 or 14 telling me about life and how important it all is. I got plenty of them as things started happening more into a negative arena of life though. How could I have known? Even today every little decision has an effect on life ahead, this of course can be a very stressful way to live, worrying about what might become out of how or what I choose now. So as a young teenager I definitely missed the class or that day in school where the lesson was about consequences of actions or the follow on effect of good or bad choices.

Mind you, I did not do a lot of schooling, I walked out of the place at a very young age, so does it make sense that dropping out of school at 12 or 13 years of age that a path to prison is inevitable?

SCHOOL DAYS.

School and me were always a fantastic couple, I loved the social aspect of school from as far back as I could remember. The lessons or the studying were not difficult at all and many times I enjoyed that I could get the answers right, without too much thought. Something in learning made the world seem right to me as a child, learning was fun and easy and I do know that was not the same for everyone but back then I really thought it was that easy for everyone. As I got closer to leaving the early years of school at ten and eleven I was already being a sneaky child. My grades were always in the high percentages with marks of A's and B's and if I saw a grade of C for something I would be a little upset inside. Sneaky though, yes, I had started smoking cigarettes and had a number of episodes of drinking alcohol, one of which I shared with you earlier. So yes by such an early age I had begun using my brains not only for my studies and getting good grades but also to outwit or outsmart the adults. I was young and saw that being smart meant keeping it all hid and nobody could find out. What is it or how does it become that the path to deviousness is entertaining to a young boy? I do understand you may be a girl reading this and / or may have a daughter but I can only explain it as a boy. It is like when we dress a child and tell them not to get their clothes dirty, is it that we should never have suggested it in the first place? Like never have planted the seed by placing the words clothes and dirt in the same sentence. Definitely there is something in that, the more the adults said no, the more I looked for a way to carry on regardless. If a teacher had sat me down at ten years old and said "look we know you like a bit of craic and divilment, but smoking and drinking and trying to outsmart the adults is going to lead you to a prison cell before you reach the age of twenty" would I have listened anyway? Did my young head which was great at reproducing study material, did it have the capacity to understand?

Like I said, I enjoyed school, I enjoyed learning and all the fun with my friends both in and outside of the classroom, something inside of me did not like the limitations, to have restrictions placed upon me was like a red rag to a bull. I did not charge at the authority figure who may have administered the orders, I would more like, tip toe along casually and cross the boundary lines in my own little cool way. For some reason in the summer of my twelfth year in life everything changed and starting secondary school that year brought about some serious changes to my whole attitude.

School just wasn't for me any more. Smoking at my break times and drinking alcohol on the weekends were more the focus and this little chap who enjoyed learning so much had all come to a stop. I still got great satisfaction from knowing all the answers but me and my schooling years were coming to a halt and quickly at that.

Why did I not want to stay in school anymore?

Why did I not want to behave in class anymore?

Why did my teachers represent blockades to me?

Why did I want to fool my parents? By ducking out of school.

Why did hearing any adults advice just not register?

To all of the above I have very little excuse. I can say with all sincerity that alcohol and being a young boy were very clearly the wrong mix. I wanted to be free and I wanted to live the way I saw fit. Consequences meant nothing to me and no other person was going to change my mind. Why or how could they? I was very much my own little person and for sure the rebel that nobody was going to order around. Though being an independent minded child does not lead straight to prison, having opinions and thinking to know it all as a teenager does not bring about a blazing trail or a direct line to the prison gates.

SVENTEEN & EMBARRASSED

If not then what, I hear you ask and rightfully so. I Have spent the whole night so far, tossing and turning wrecking my own head asking the same question. What brings one to a position of looking out from behind bars? It is easy for you to form some opinions, maybe feel like the answers must be blatantly obvious, I assure you there are many a young boy who are in the process of thinking my exact thoughts right now who cannot find the oh so easily presumable answer either.

There have been so many times as a young boy that being innocent was and they still are the sweetest memories I carry with me. Not the innocence that had been needed when facing the judge of the court. The naivety that comes with being young, so it has to be the most perfect and natural that life can be. Maybe you are a teenager yourself right now and if not then you can recall being one. Did you think the world is cruel? Did you think that getting embarrassed easily was like the end of the world? Or maybe even like me you may have just thought life, along with all it's fun, beauty & freedom would and could go on forever.

Seventeen and Life

As an adult or as a teenager what really is the difference between how we feel about our lives and what may ever become? If you are a parent who has a young child, perhaps you can check in with them regularly and help them in making the breakthrough from childhood naivety into all of a slap adult life and adult rules. It does not mean that every quiet shy child will grow out of it nor does it mean every strong minded child is heading for a prison cell, like where I have found myself tonight. Nah! Not at all. I should really rephrase that last piece, no "it doesn't mean" the real, real I do not mean it to be or to sound like anything is as simple or clean cut and dry like that. There are the possibilities of anything turning out to be anything, really.

Look at the teenage years, becoming an official teenager is a milestone we have all passed through. Leaving 12 behind us forever and we became thirteen, unlucky for some (you might just rattle that off every time you see 13). I remember the morning it happened for me. I was given a card and a greeting of well done from my mother. What exactly was that about? I had just entered the single most confusing time of any young boy's life and I get a well done. What was that, some sort of secret code word greeting to life's next level or even a welcome to the club of early adulthood where everything you thought was fun and cool just got a whole lot more complicated. Teenage years, I had arrived to a new place in life where now I receive a "well done" for getting older.....

If I belonged to a tribe in Africa, I would be getting special gloves filled with ants that bite and seeing if I can withstand their sting all night long while my female counterpart gets her hair plucked one by one til bald. A day later with hands more tender than a diaper rash and to be led by my elders to meet my now new wife to be who has been plucked bald all night by the women of the tribe. Yeah becoming a teenager has its perks alright......

But here I am, could be that if anyone wants to tell the truth to children about it, well let's just see in a few words or so, (of course I am limited to a boy's perspective)

Acne, horrible greasy spots that are going to appear in and around your face with no warning and it will never matter what diet you try to keep.

Puberty, this is a whole other series of books to be written. But there is the portion of hair that might start growing between your legs, what on earth is this mess? The hair that will grow from your armpits and not just look ugly but stink like fuck at the absolute wrong times always. While on the subject of hair, this idea of hair growing out of your face, well, this is the most embarrassing of all as if it grows it won't grow right and is a reason for your friends to make fun of you. Then if none grows from around your face, this again is a reason, yup! You guessed it, a reason for your friends to make fun of you.

Seventeen and Life

Erections, yes I know for the ladies you cannot understand these but we don't have a clue about breasts so evens us up there a little. Anyway these things start popping off all over the place. Wake up with one, walk into school with one and it has nothing to do with seeing girls or fantasies, they just show up, you could be deep in a science class learning about the Pangaea and up it will come. No warnings and the bell goes and you have to stand up and walk out in some way, shape or form that nobody can notice. If another boy notices, major embarrassment. If a girl notices, well just shoot me now and be done.

Of course there are many more that deserve mention

Hair, everywhere & greasy.

Voice, deepening & broken.

Hormones, sometimes want to be that little doggy that dry humps everybody's leg.

Seventeen and Life

The list keeps on going, to say this is a time "milestone of life changing" to be welcomed to, has to be a joke?

Can I figure why becoming a teenager is such a great time and what it is to be in the era of rites of passage? No not really. And stuck at seventeen to make it all only worse, rightly stuck. Locked up with nowhere to go, my only way out of a prison cell will be by the turn of a key from a prison guard who is only doing his job. Does he care I am a young boy or, okay fair enough a young man then. Does it even make a difference to him? A young man with the emotional intelligence of a ten year old kid.

A teenager, the time in life of a quincenera or the sweet sixteen birthday party. A time when turning eighteen brings you into full on adulthood, the entering with a welcome you are now a teenager at 13 followed swiftly by you are now 18 and full grown responsible adult. Everything is legal by eighteen. Special birthday party thrown for the ages 15 & 16, everything so wonderful and cute and child like, then again at 18 the big birthday bash to celebrate becoming an adult and now legally able to vote etc etc, so what happened to 17? Who decided that this can be the all forgotten about year? All the pressures of life and just left hanging in the wind.

The title of this book "Seventeen & Life" kind of gives it all away really, at seventeen years of age I did not know anything about anything really yet the trials and tribulations of life were starting to slap me around the face just a little bit too hard. How could I know every little choice I had made was the build up to being an "inmate" to give me my official new title, prisoner 47862, nice name isn't it? The crossroads had appeared like it had been air dropped into the fast lane of a freeway, the autobahn where there are no speed limits.

Seventeen, the year to begin dabbling in sewing wild oats, learn to dance in rhythm with a female partner. Know what you are ready to do as a career for the rest of your life. Study hard and enjoy every minute of it, learn all there is left in the text books. Voice that new found opinion of yours in adult conversations. Yes this is the take off year, the steady taxiing along the largest runway you have ever faced to date. Yes this is the year where it all is going to miraculously change, the preparation year of life, maybe even be given permission to indulge in a few pints of beer at a family function. Quite possibly the year when you are taken out for a few sneaky driving lessons by your father or your mother. This is it! Sweet sixteen is behind you, "check rear-view mirror" life of all kinds of freedom lies ahead, "eyes forward at all times". For now you are permitted or it is okay to call over and spend time hanging out with your girlfriend while she is babysitting, the family do not mind, "they will be fine, they are 17 and so mature for their age"

Oh yes, this is the pinnacle of your teenage years, now I have to bring it up and remind you that only 4, yes that is right four short years ago you turned or became a teenager for the first time and now at seventeen you are being handed responsibilities left, right & centre. You are not fully permitted to do anything legally yet and the chomping at the bit is getting harder to hide.

When really, let's be honest about it here, what would we rather be doing? Getting stuck into fully understanding the naked body, both that of the girls and even our own. Testing the waters across the vast arenas. Smoking cigarettes til our head spins, we puke and say to ourselves "nope definitely not for me". Get a little drunk with our friends, we puke and say to ourselves "that was fun, I hated the puking part but I am gonna be better at it next time". Kissing your girlfriend and really getting into the passionate tongue wrestling part of spit swapping, no household, not hers or yours are allowing a bedroom to sleep together yet and all you keep saying to yourself whilst with her, "touch it, touch it, touch it. Gentle now, not too hard, not too soft. Ah Fuck! Never mind"

There is a lot going on in a mind at seventeen and because you have not quite hit that eighteen mark just yet, treated like a child by society. Although all the laws support 18 as if to have undergone some major metamorphosis in an almost overnight fashion.

I mentioned to you a little earlier about the awkwardness of being totally embarrassed as being such a major part of life as a child, well yes this never really left me. Could it have been me learning about anxiety and being anxious or just a normal kid who found being embarrassed as being a little too intense? Who knows what or where it came from, the feeling had stayed with me from a young age and still existed at 17. When I was smaller about eight or so I was in the cub-scouts. I loved wearing the uniform and took great pride in ironing my neckerchief and never gave a single thought to how ridiculous I looked. So really if it didn't cross my mind I didn't get embarrassed but this one time my father had bought me my shoes for the year ahead and, they were like mans shoes, I loved them as they were tipped with steel tips on the heels, to last longer of course. I thought they were great, oxblood was the colour of them and when I walked out of that shoe shop with those bad boys on, they could have been pink with light green spots on them. They had steel tips on them and I was click clicking away as I walked down the street with my dad to his car, I was walking the street in the big city of Dublin with a man's pair of shoes on and sounded like a true man clicking with every step. These new shoes were the business.

Before scouts would start in the evenings we would be there a little earlier than start time and get some play time ahead of our scout meeting in our prefabricated building "scout den". This was always cool because none of my classmates were in the scouts with me and so it was a whole different group of friends, this was cool too until the night I showed up with my new oxblood coloured new shoes. I over heard one the guys saying "look at his red shoes" to me they were oxblood colour and nothing else. When we were called into the den and every body was lined up and I had to walk across the floor in front of everyone, I wanted to die, all I could think was people are looking at my shoes and calling them red at which point halfway across the floor my face probably was too.

That feeling of embarrassed that came from deep in the abyss of my stomach, filling me all the way up. Oh trust me when I tell you that not only would my face go red but out to the most pointed tip of my ears would be burning, roasting even and I wanted the world to stop. Self conscious to the maximum and just the worst way to feel, ever.

I did not know what to do in those situations, how to act was beyond my thinking. It is like as if the single most difficult thing I would have to do ever was feel embarrassed. I made up lies at home that we needed to wear running shoes to scout meetings and anything else I could think of to try and get out of wearing these what I not only days earlier thought were the best thing since slice bread, now they just represented super, major self conscious embarrassment OVERLOAD and for what?

This embarrassing feeling has to be the single most awkward thing ever, like where does it even come from? Feelings of all types come from somewhere inside of us, obviously I can get my head around that, to a point of understanding. But when I think about It a little more my questions get real tricky to even understand for myself. To be embarrassed! For a moment in time, face getting red and the feeling heat under the collar. Items around you drift out of focus, people around somehow are peering at you more intensely now. The more red your cheeks become the hotter it gets, sweaty armpits, hands and even neck and shoulders, the groin too. No body part is safe from this rush that is taking over the body. I Have never known how to act, where to look or how to just be. Does my getting embarrassed over the stupidest little thing bring about more emotions? Another head scratcher for me, is it coupled with some sort of anxiousness too? Having a slight anxiety attack due to an overload of embarrassment. I knew my emotion of being embarrassed showed on my face and I knew people could see me clearly but this was something more than that, I thought they were seeing me as paper thin and they were or could see inside of me, somewhere into the depths of my emotion's manufacturing plant. Now they knew every little private inch of my being. Yes I am talking a hyper sensitive side to me which is my absolute private place. For a moment of an embarrassment could lead me to be a runaway, in my mind I had already bolted out the door. These feelings were not only strange to me but also so new. Feelings about which I knew nothing about, the mere existence brought about all the covering up and pretending, I did not want any feelings to just pop up. It always came from nowhere and felt the most private thing to me, how I feel was nobody's business!

I am talking late eighties and early nineties when I was a kid and at home or in school seemed to carry a similar lesson, don't answer back or receive extra punishment. In school we used to get what we called "lines" as punishment, something like "I must not speak in class" and our orders were to write it out one hundred or two hundred times. The reckoning was, a sore wrist from the writing may just be enough to keep a child more focused and of course less disruptive in a classroom. I think it was in 1988 we had a teacher who would appear to be losing his mind when giving out lines as a punishment, his were like the record breakers, the clever bastard knew that we would write the lines all in a row down the page. Start off with I , I , I all the way down the left and then must, must, must. NOT, NOT, NOT....& so on, this was a method we would write so as to just get them done. The message of what we had done wrong in class that day completely ignored. So this particular teacher of ours that year would tell us to copy down our lines from the chalkboard and off he would go,

When I find myself in class and a little bored, I will not speak with or make any attempts to distract any of my fellow classmates. My classmates are here to learn and have no desire to hear me or any of my disruptions..

100 times of having to write those kind of lines made talking in class seem just not worth the headaches.

However what exactly is all the school years about ? Have I really been so naive that I never figured out, all the academic learning was so useless. That is a tough thing to say, I know, it is more along the lines of how I disagree with the schooling system and how children are thought all the skills needed to become a "bubble blower" in a soap factory or gain the perfect skills to take note after note, where are the life skills? Where was the day in school that thought me, well let's imagine for a moment, your school teacher walks into your class one morning and says this "good morning kids, books and notebooks away, today we are going to begin learning about life" okay so kids would not want to listen anyway, he continues "we are going to begin with the first step, how to spot an asshole"

Would the kids start paying attention then?

Possibly because the word asshole was used, then yes children may pay attention to a school teacher who is about to get real with them. Start talking about real life in school.

I could have been singled out and brought to the front of my classroom that day. The teacher would have said, "Today class we are going to discuss what Aidan should do through his teenage years, so that he can be very certain that he will avoid going to prison". I never sat in a classroom where this kind of thing was discussed, nope not ever. I am using this as an example of course.

There were no lessons as a child to discuss things like that or if you can trace back your own memory of school days as a young child, did your teacher ever teach you about how to spot any personality types in people? Were there any lessons ever thought to you that came along the lines of, "here is how to identify early in life, the type of person who will take pleasure in lying about you" No! I didn't think so. The reason we cannot recall these types of life lessons is because they did not happen. Nobody ever pulled me to the side in school and explained to me what it means when another human being bullies another human being.

I can safely say that had I gotten any of these kinds of lessons, perhaps and I am only thinking aloud here to say maybe I might have made a few better choices and could have saved myself the trip to right where I am right now.

There is only one way to learn about life and the people in it. Some of us make mistakes and learn from them and some of the rest of us continue to repeatedly keep on making the same mistakes over and over again. Is that the individual's fault or did they just go to a very bad school?

I am not bitter about the school system that is in place and am not holding any grudges for any of my school teachers that I had the pleasure of enduring. It is just an important part of how I see some openings of what a teenager may need as a real helping hand in life, a real boost along their journey. A few simple pointers may just have been enough to help me stay clear of this damp and dreary jail cell. My first night in prison and I cannot understand with any clarity of what exactly was the trigger along my journey from child to man. What brought me to be housed under lock and key?

There are no classes for this as a young boy, it is entirely up to me to figure out who is who tomorrow morning when the latch turns on my cell door, the game begins anew. Spot the manipulator immediately, keep a keen eye out for the hustler, take no crap from the bullies. Watch out for the friendly guy, he may just be the wolf in sheep's clothing. Oh yes, when that door opens in the morning, the new school day begins. We are now firmly held or firmly housed in the true "college of Knowledge". Am I ready for this at only 17? There have been no preschool days for this college, there is no teacher tomorrow either, no safety net or anything even close. A tough world awaits me in the morning, not a nice place to be as a teenager and how could I be ready?

Is it even right that I should be stressing this way, about what lies outside of that chunk of metal, like can it be that it is thought that this prison door is what is bringing some reality into play? My freedom gone. Where I sit right now in a prison bed it is very much clear to me and by the roars and shouting coming from the other prisoners is explaining to me that my cell door is what is keeping me safe right now, never mind the whole locked in aspect. I can hear the same few voices over and over again, it is almost like the louder they shout the same threats the more intimidating it actually is.

I never learned about this kind of stuff in school and any teenager right now today probably is not learning it either. It is easy to think that a young adult should know right from wrong of course but who actually took the time to teach them? Like I had mentioned before, it is the turning of age for any teenager, once upon a time it was all fun thirteen and fourteen years of age then bang sixteen is in the rear-view mirror and seventeen is upon you. Not old enough to be a full on responsible adult yet too old to be considered a youngster any more. Seventeen and Life is the crossroads I have found myself at, is it a crossroads of the be all and end all of life or perhaps just another everyday street corner? Turn left or turn right which can be no big deal either way or, do the decisions made right now bring about the entire rest of my life and my future?

Let us go back a little earlier and dice up these schooling years some more, what have they really meant or even what do they mean to a child of seventeen? I did not stay attending school from around the age of twelve or thirteen. Yes it is not my place to speak on what may or may not be the correct way of how somethings should or should not have been as I did not attend too long and maybe missed all the life lectures.

My early departure from the routine school days probably left me with more time on my hands for mischief and less time spent coexisting with other students to watch and learn from each other. Yeah, now this is a very probable truth of the whole matter. Should a guidance person in the school be more involved with kids just like me? This is a little difficult to assess properly because I wanted to know or even maybe should have known the birds and the bees at about 8 and a trading and marketing crash course by somewhere around 14. But here is to the woulda, coulda, shoulda. In my looking back, it is definitely a schooling error, however the error is on me. I did not stick around long enough to learn more about life nor did I think the people teaching us knew much about it either, I wanted to be free, out in the world with nobody telling me what to do, just out there making my own mistakes.

Is it fair that parents expect us to learn everything and more from our school teachers. A crèche for big kids really, isn't it? Is it okay to drop off a child at school at the age of twelve and by the time they are eighteen and coming out the other end, be like "WTF" who has my child become? It would seem to me that the school years are valuable then, two fold really, children growing up into teenagers learning from their peers not only by interacting with each other as friends but also watching those who maybe are not their friends, watching how to act socially and stacking up on some extra learned behaviours.

Along with the educational aspect of schooling, the teenage years are definitely the difficult ones. Why not make the whole schooling and the teenage era a threefold time, learn from peers and teachers alike, the educational benefits coupled with the social interacting skills all coupled with some parental involvement. A little time taken to cherish the years but also be a big part of the growing element of life, emotional development. What good is being the brain box in school with 100% scores in every test the academics throw at you if there are no friends to play with or the class clown with poor grades but is ever so popular with all the other kids. Hard to find a middle isn't it, add in some parental involvement to where responsibilities are added year after year and maybe by seventeen things could be on a bit of a balance.

WHAT ABOUT COPS ?

Again the, 17 years of age conundrum, what is a teenager at seventeen supposed to know about life?

Sitting in a jail cell at only seventeen brings about many thoughts, where did it all go wrong? What is this treat me like an adult caper? What has lead me to this point, a crossroads of where I must change direction, a junction in life where things must change. Change for the better of course, what good can it be if I choose the wrong path from here and just continue downhill. I must try and identify what series of choosing the wrong path has lead me to be held under lock and key. If I can find the link to it all then I can adjust accordingly and make right, now only seventeen there is plenty of time left to bring about the better side of me as a person, this night here is a low point that can serve as the beginning to something way more special in my life, or life as a whole thing.

You can take it from me that jail is not somewhere you ever want to find yourself and so if you think you are in a bad place now, well it can always get worse. It might always be worth having a little think about what to do in any given situation. All our choices bring us to turn corners and meander our way through our own story of life. Though when still not an adult at seventeen our choices play a huge part and our word is taken as a full grown man or woman so better use some thought process in making those decisions.

Seventeen and Life

Leads to a very good topic of discussion though, the whole responsibility for our actions and our choices.

I am here tonight in a prison cell, neighbours, my new neighbours that is of course, are all criminals and basically made some pretty bad choices along their own path in life so far. I wonder as to what exactly is it that they might have been thinking when they were only seventeen. Here is an even bigger question, what were you thinking at seventeen?

Has your life changed because of what you did back then and what it is now because of your teenage decisions or can you even remember? Do we know what life is all about as a teenager and if we can honestly with hand on heart say that there is no way a teenager can have any real clue about the world and any deeper meaning to life, then why expect so much of such a young person? Isn't there plenty of time for grown up stuff when they are grown up.

It is hard enough for a young boy or girl to have to figure out their peers and "peer pressure" walk through the battlefields of school and social gatherings, what with bullies lurking on every corner. The popular kids, the straight up hurtful kids and they are only teenagers themselves, how can we expect that the youngsters doing the bullying even know what they are doing?

Let's add into the mix all the feelings and emotions that are now becoming a major if not major perhaps absolute gigantic part of a teenagers life. Feeling socially awkward and going into themselves to build strategies and coping skills of how to navigate the battlefields mentioned above.

Anyone who is reading this right now is either one of two groups, you are currently a teenager and know exactly what I am talking about and how it is or you are an adult and you have crossed through your teenage years and can remember exactly what it was like for you. Please don't as an adult say

Seventeen and Life

"Oh I just don't understand the kids these days" if that is your stance then perhaps you learned a great coping skill of your own back when you were just a simple teenager which was to blur it out and forget how it was. Because I firmly believe that the fact we have all passed through these years of change in our lives, we can say yes we know these experiences, yes we remember what it was like and for this simple reason it would be best served that we give a few moments thought when dealing with a teenager. Why not? We were all there once. Even though this is about as cliché as they come, it is a simple fact, the truth of once being young and growing up to somehow becoming an adult and then by miraculous transformations, becoming an adult caused some form of amnesia, a memory loss specific to all adolescent learning and of what it was like just to be young and vulnerable. Teenage years are not the almighty era of revelation that seems to be hinted at by all those that have gone before me, the majority of adults who speak down to me now have just some how, have forgotten the years of being seventeen.

Why is it such a significant year, what makes it so special, following on from "sweet sixteen" the new era of seventeen could be known as "special seventeen".

The decisions we are faced with as a teenager can or could shape the entire rest of our lives. Imagine, here I am, a teenager with very limited knowledge about anything in life at all yet the choices I make now can shape my very future. What sort of a raw deal is that, it is like handing a five year old your credit card and telling them, "go and buy our family a car". And of course, do you know why we don't send our five year olds out car shopping, well it has something to do with, IT DOESN'T WORK! Kind of thing.

Seventeen and Life

Now that we have started scratching the surface of what can and cannot be, well let's just say "fair", on a teenager. I wonder given my current predicament where being honest might get me now. I always remember maybe even like a thousand times that "honesty will get you everywhere" well I need to get places and they definitely have nothing to do with being here in prison, so my wondering about what role honesty and being honest are going to get me. Or more to a point of thought, what is being honest in the first place? Go out there tomorrow morning and tell them I am sorry for all events leading up to and the most recent that have led me to be locked up. Is this the honesty that they have been harping on about? This kind of display of honesty from me would be genuine and a real testament of how I feel inside, guilt driven yes this is true, but I do not know any other form of honesty.

What is being honest in life? I will say that my honesty has probably gotten me into more trouble and problems than it has ever gotten me out of.

Example, I was asked one time in a school classroom by the teacher, well to clarify it was not just a random question, I had been a bit disruptive to the class by talking and so the teacher wanted to make an example out of me and she asked me a question, "do you think I come here to have to shout over you? A pupil, is it that you believe I am someone you do not have to show respect to? What exactly do You think I am? "

So I answered as honestly as I could, I thought only for a few moments and replied, "miss I think it is a waste of time, yes you are wasting your time and ours and there is a horrible smell off of you" this was as honest as I could have been. This got me in quite a bit of trouble.

Seventeen and Life

I had been one night in an altercation with another young guy, well I hit him a few times over a stupid argument we were having. To me at the time it was a stupid argument and the way to finish it was to throw a few punches, a bit stupid of me I know but a young guy like me did not really know how to get my point across without firing my fists into action and so he had received or been injured with a bit of a bloody nose and a bloodied face. No this was not the honesty piece of the night, when the police arrived they wanted to know what had happened to the guys face, I had whispered to him warning him that if he didn't want some more of a beating he would be very careful what he told the police. He told them that he had fallen and it was no big deal, he said he was a little bit drunk and that he had been clumsy enough to fall over. To this the police had more questions "we got a call from someone there was a fight and we don't believe you just fell, so why not tell us who did this and we will take care of it from there"

My turn to become honest as I saw it, I rolled or swaggered up to the front "you heard what the guy said, he fell! Why not go and find some real crime and leave us alone"

The police did not appreciate my remarks and of course I was only fifteen at the time so I would have come across as a very cheeky and daring young fella altogether. Their response "we are not talking to you so why don't you keep your mouth shut"

Now this would make my blood boil and bring on my honesty a little stronger "excuse me! This is a free country and I can speak where and when I want to. You are not the law you are peace keepers employed to keep the peace, not stick your chest and tell me to shut up"

The policeman responded quite sharply "alright then I am arresting you for a breach of the peace, under section blah blah blah blah...." So once again speaking my mind and being as honest as I could had gotten me arrested.

Seventeen and Life

Now one could argue that I had started a fight with a guy and so to be arrested was only fair. How and ever I was not placed under arrest for assaulting the poor guy, nor for being abusive in any way to the police, I was arrested for speaking my mind and giving my honest opinion as I saw it. So this is just another example of how in my own innocence that I found out that giving my honest opinion of or in the middle of a situation was a direct path slash recipe for problems and trouble.

Given these couple of examples and of how I thought of what being honest was all about, I definitely had developed a strange sense of what exactly did being honest mean. How can a young boy know these things? Seriously, like what? What exactly are they looking for when they say honesty is the best policy?

Let's see exactly, I am sitting in a prison cell, there are rodents running around the kip at my feet and to think the worst has yet to come. In the morning I have to go and mix with some of these lunatics I can hear howling away all their threats to each other. Is this an honest account of my situation?

It is about as simple as I can break things down right now so it must be "the" honest run down alright. I have been dishonest to lead me here in the first place, I have broken the law somewhere along the line and "locked up" here is my punishment. This really seems like the here and now of it all.

I wonder can you actually imagine this?

WHAT IS "Honest" ?

Of course there is a whole different level of honesty that perhaps we should take a look at. The honesty that I have learned might actually mean something, something that nobody has ever bothered to teach me about. I have never been explained to about nor ever heard anyone speak of. Why have or has everyone kept this secret from me. Why as a teenager does one have to figure all this shit out for themselves. Yes the honesty. What is it I am rambling on about you might ask yourself right about now too, well, the real honest piece of me, to get honest with myself.

Yes I am in a prison cell and yes indeed there are nut cases yelling at each other right outside of my door, all this is true but the real truth and my get real and honest with myself comes down to my very own feelings. Ooops! There I have said it. Feelings, what are these things that no-one has ever mentioned to me before. I am sitting in my cell, scared. I am way past nervous and I have the deepest of guilt. So all these feelings, what are these? Where are they coming from and what part do they play in honesty?

Where did I ever learn to be scared would be a good question to start with. What is this being nervous? Why does an honesty of how I am actually feeling seem to be the most real thing ever to have occurred in my life so far. These feelings are very real and are a direct result of my whereabouts, my total and really undeniable surroundings. The echoes in the hallways and well more so how the shouting rings across the landings of the prison block, the fluorescent lighting coming in under my door, you know the kind, the type of lighting you find, probably only find in one of three places. Hospital waiting rooms, the waiting area of the accident and emergency department of the hospitals or here on the inside of a prison cell block or lastly the entrance and reception area of a morgue. The lights being too bright yet dull, what a contradiction though it is so true, a dreary type of lighting. So my question on this point is in wondering how the lighting actually is affecting my mood or is it that when we feel certain things does our complete viewpoint change?

The three places I just mentioned are never associated with happy times, we do not feel happy in any of those three places and so due to our feelings, is it for this reason that makes these settings drab and dreary? Because of how I am feeling is how I see my surroundings, this would have to mean that my brain and the pupils of my eyes are constructing a different kind of image based upon my feelings, this would have to go down as being my first ever experience of mindfulness. To understand what it is that is going on in my life and this understanding corresponding at the precise time and place with my own feelings and emotions. Or of course as any of you might just be able to imagine, my first night in prison and it feels like "shit".

I can spend all of my time here in prison wondering what exactly lead me here and trying to piece together all of the finest of details from my childhood to see if there is something that will show me the error of my ways, if even only a little idea to better help me to make some changes to me, myself. Or I can focus on what is happening right now and how I feel and what it is that I must do to make changes to my very own character and the person I think that I am to the person I actually am.

Is this the real purpose of prison? The place for reflection and self realization or why can such things not just be thought to teenagers from an early age and save any young man a trip to the courts and the shackles that are placed on him as he is lead away to his prison cell.

Yes being honest, "honesty is the key that will set you free" so an honest account to myself about my feelings. Is this the "be true to yourself" that which I have heard mentioned before. And to go back and think some more about what is the connection between how we view something when we are feeling any particular way. Like I said about the miserable lighting in three horrible locations, all of which are not good places to have to spend any time in. So what is the process our brain goes through in processing the images we see with our very own eyes. How can our vision change due to how we feel?

I can remember being in the mountains on two separate occasions, there is plenty of forest land in the mountains which are located just to the south of the city of Dublin. I was there as a child camping with my father and my brothers. It was a nice weekend, the weather was warm and very summer like. We had built a raft for the river over the weekend and we did plenty of swimming too. Each night we cooked and sat around the fire until our eyes were struggling to stay open, we always had the fire going to help keep some smoke in the air around our camp. We were camping at the bottom of a hill, kind of a meadow type field which ended down to the river. The flat area where we had our tent pitched was a couple of feet from the river bank and only another few feet away the river bend had created a big natural pool, where there was an area of river sand that made the perfect little beach.

The woods were the far side of the river and more woods to the top of the meadow. The river was quite easy to cross at either end or the larger pool area as it did narrow in again at each side and was only like a foot deep across these sections. The water was a murky brown but not cloudy like, more like water that had been dyed or something but then when in it and swimming you could see your feet walking across the river rocks below. From the beach or the bank it was hard to see anything below the surface of the water due to the brownish taint that it had. We fished in that river and we swam to our hearts content. Plus with the great raft our father built for us meant we were either in the brown river water or on top of it paddling our raft around the natural pool that had formed on this particular part of the river bend.

Seventeen and Life

We wandered around the woods too a couple of the afternoons and we would keep shouting out to each other every so often. Even though I remember wandering around alone and feeling amazing to be in the woods free and alone, mind you I did know my brothers were not too far away at any given time. So the few days spent up the mountains with our father was really something picture perfect in a sense, we swam all day, when not wet we wandered the hills and the forests and our chores were to gather firewood from the forest floors so that on our return, the fire side was well stocked for the night ahead and the cooking to come. It was a very real little house on the prairie type time spent camping with our father and for these simple reasons of it being so wonderful and my feelings at that time being all good and energetic, just like any young boy on a camping trip with his brothers and father.

Is it for all the nice feelings that helps to keep this memory simple and pure in my mind? I was about eight years of age those summer months and it definitely is a memory that has lived on, of a "niceness" about Ireland and what the mountains and forest truly have to offer us. The memory of course on a camping trip with Dad, how could it hold anything else other than fond memories and to tie this back to what I was getting at earlier, my feelings of that time spent camping in the mountains were happy and free and loving along with feeling safe and secure because my dad was in charge. So my eyes saw everything nicely, I remember the colours of the forest being all mixed from greens and yellows to browns and deeper greens too, red and some black where branches had fallen and left those black marks right where they had split at the bow. All of these colours I can still picture them, the main feeling that arises from this memory and all these colours is that I feel warm. I can recall it like yesterday and it brings a happy smile to my mind and sometimes the feeling can be stronger when I recall and a smile can even happen across my face. So my eyes or my minds eye remembers being secure and happy, free to have fun as a young child. This would mean to me that due to my happy feelings at that time, my memory is a happy one and how I remembered all the colours to be nice and beautiful, due to my perception at the time based on happy feelings surrounding the memory everything remains beautiful and wonderful in my memory.

I went back and revisited this exact same place a few years later with my life long friend Kenneth, he had been researching the concept of prospecting for gold in rivers and he had mapped out some locations based upon his research and so called geological formations within the mountain range just south of Dublin, we headed off one morning early with his van fully loaded with everything a novice gold prospector would need and a few tools on the advanced side too.

It was a good start because Kenneth never liked to do anything by half measures, we had sleeping bags so that we could camp out just in case we struck the mother load, he had also in the van some gold pans for panning and a couple of shovels and pick axes "for shifting some sand and small rocks" he said. We also had a few buckets to keep the gold in when we clean out the sluice box, which was not that large about four or five feet long, he also said that the dredge nozzle and the Honda engine are just for when we hit "pay dirt".

It was only when we got to the wooded area at the top of the hill, that's the hill that is the grass land meadow like area above the river. This is the meadow that carried some great memories of mine, rolling in it from top to bottom and chasing the summer bees from butter cup to butter cup. The great summer camp with my father and the freedom roaming the hillsides and the forests. It was at this moment with Kenneth on the very same hill that I was not enjoying it, sweat dripping off my back and my feet soaked from the marshy ground beneath me. The heavy mountain mist, well really rain like mist that was soaking my clothes too, my clothes soaking on the outside from the mist and soaking on the inside from my own sweat. Huffing and puffing I continued with a hose for the dredge draped around my shoulders and both hands full with shovels and buckets and steel mesh for the sluice box. I was looking down the hill at him as he was blazing a trail for the river, he kept looking back and saying "we will drop this stuff and go back up and get the rest of it in a minute"

Same hill as my fond memories, same person which is me and a completely different outlook now. I got to the river bank like a work horse on his last legs, I plonked down all the equipment and said "fuck this place man, there is no way I am going back up there for more shit, I am going to rest here and you go if you want. I will mind our stuff here just in case anyone comes along".

We had enough equipment to start a mining corporation and this was only a trial run just to do a bit of prospecting. My view point had all of a sudden changed about that hill and the woods above. There was steam coming from my chest somewhere and my breath was making like full on smoke as I exhaled each gasp and puff. Good old Kenneth though, off he went for more stuff and I remained perched on the one rock that sat half buried in the sand of the river shore. This is the exact same rock I used to jump and dive from as a kid. I reached down a hand to feel the water and it was as cold as ice, still brown though, just absolutely freezing. Come to think of it nothing much had changed about the entire area, my feelings had changed that day and due to circumstances and how my eyes were seeing it, more importantly my mind's eye.

I am using the example to demonstrate how based upon surroundings and how we feel in them is how we humans can develop a sense of where we are and what we are doing all into a memory based on our feelings. It is our feelings that will shape our perception and so just like the prison lighting or the morgue or the emergency room waiting area, they have a shitty ass memory for us due to how we were feeling whilst there. This here would represent some major breakthrough for me in learning about LIFE! If we can possess the ability to get enthusiastic about where ever we are going or find a contentment in our here and now surroundings no matter what the situation is, we may just uncover the key to a happier more enjoyable life.

This my friends is a way in finding our path to a true happiness. All based alone on how we focus our minds eye without our feelings allowing our mind to become closed due to a negative feeling of any sorts taking us over. We do possess the ability to feel and we also possess the ability to make a decision on what we can do with how we feel.

How or what does change mean to you?

Words can be funny that way, I have noticed a lot, how depending on what is going on for you or what is happening in your day is exactly what will shape how you see things or how your meaning for anything will form. So we can say for example, the word "change" it will totally depend on where your mind is at, at this very moment you are reading this, yes right now say to yourself CHANGE !

A woman who decided to go shopping for the day and who had a wonderful time swanning around the shops, walking into department stores and boutiques alike all to enjoy the attentive store workers who helped her pick and choose some great outfits for her night out tonight with her new boyfriend. Date night number three this will be for the new couple. The lady has spent the day trying on outfits that not only made her look stunningly beautiful but were affordable to her budget also, what a win win for her and a great way to spend her life that day. She has enjoyed the feel of new clothes and to look at herself in the mirror in the stores was so amazing to her eyes that she just had to buy maybe just a little more than she had first planned for that day.

Being that this particular day just so happened to be a Wednesday, the shops in her city were quiet enough and had fewer shoppers than normal so it made for the easiest of days to wander from shop to shop, her lunch in the cafe atop the department store over looking the city, no waiting in line with her tray behind a hungry lunch mob. When she entered the ladies fashions floor, she was greeted immediately by a store employee who was only too happy to help. Her time spent with the girl working in the women's department today also sharing in a little joy of having a quieter day with a little fewer customers than normal. The two spent a happy afternoon together, one woman seeing herself all dressed up with new clothes and tags to tear off in excitement when she gets home, not only excited for having spent her hard earned money on herself but also excited for the new feelings of falling in love that have been going on in her life too.

The second woman is the staff member at the store, she had maybe a little tougher morning preparing her children for school, getting the lunches packed while making sure they had eaten their breakfast. A little more hurried if she was to make the commuter train into the city that day. She had ran to catch it and was a few coins short for her ticket at the machine. She had to fumble around for a note in her purse, a little panicked too as the train was at the platform and boarding quickly too. "Come on, come on stupid machine" as she waited for all the coins to drop down into the tray of the machine so she could run the twenty or thirty feet to board the 8.45 to the city that morning. The two women were definitely having different kinds of a Wednesday for sure, yet for this afternoon they shared their laughs together as one of them slipped in and out of different dresses, different in style and colour and of most notably, different in price. Whilst the other lady was running to the store rooms for larger sizes and smaller sizes for her new customer to try on. The differences are obvious alright and to each at any given moment a word can mean something so different, to our young woman who is full of enthusiasm and excitement for her date night to which if we drop the word "change" on her it runs through her mind in reference to clothes and outfits. What will she wear tonight and should she try on another shade of the same dress. Should she change out of the one she is liking the look of in the store mirror, the idea of chopping and changing outfits will more than likely stick with her all evening up to the point that she finally settles for a look that she is comfortable with and turns the key in her door to head out for her evening. CHANGE.

Our lovely shop assistant or sales lady in the department store is having a different day and when it comes time to ring up her customer at the till, her words will be about change, not of the same meaning. She will open the till and fumble her fingers for "change" (coins) handing back to the lady her receipt with "here is your CHANGE, your receipt & have nice day". This sales lady from the very beginning of her day has been fumbling for coins since her train commute this morning. It is highly possibly she will be offering another customer their change in a matter of moments and continue doing so throughout the remainder of her day.

Two women sharing the same moment in life together, the exact time spent together, yet one word means a whole and other something to each of them. The word change, is and of course has a few different meanings but here using the two different women as an example is just a way to highlight how depending on any person's day how a word can mean something so different to them individually. I do get this and I wonder do you? It is a way in all of our daily lives that things can be said and then heard and end up being misunderstood. One simple word can mean two completely different things to two completely different people. It is of course a huge reason that when we speak we might even consider to think and be clear in our words and deliver our thoughts clearly.

CHANGE ! For me, right now in my life, some sort of change is needed. I definitely am in need of a change of scenery. I could use a change of address for sure and last but not least which of course would be the most significant of all changes, I need to make changes to myself. I am in prison for some terrible actions on my part, there is nobody else to blame and it is probably that I have seen no wrong in my carry on and have gone about with a reckless attitude to life in general to just end up here. The change that is needed in my life is obviously major and it must come from within. It takes a prison cell and some serious reflection to figure some of this out. I never thought about changes before. I never thought all my actions were wrong nor did I think for a single second that what I did on any given day was wrong, incorrect or anything outside of just normal growing up.

I really want to ask you now at this point in our journey, what does CHANGE mean for you?

I have fucked up, there is no two ways to look at it. Seventeen and locked up, what exactly does one do now? Is it worth it to become all holy and saintly and make attempts to begin again. Who is going to believe I can be the person I always was. How can the real me just step outside of myself and say hi to the world. Is it all possible to begin again and start over? I want to identify the problem and if I can find where it all took a wrong turn so to speak, then maybe I can make the necessary adjustments to my own self and this would be or could be the happiest I could ever be. For some they seek refuge in religion, others just never change and many others don't ever even try. If I begin to imagine a future for myself then I can live it, this sounds pretty simple alright although right now I am imagining standing in line in MCDONALD'S ordering a big Mac meal, it is not happening and so power of thought and imagination does have its limitations. More like a dream really, a touch of a little non reality to throw into my first night in prison. Might as well have a few dreams too, I might not be able to sleep but that shouldn't stop me from having a little dream.

I have always had a winner's mentality and my determination had grown from a very young age. Again I can recall or blame or eventual chalk it down to my innocence. When I was a very young boy I believed the older men who were our team coaches in sports. They sometimes even yelled at us to have a focused mind. "Determination is the key to winning this match" this was driven into our young minds in the changing rooms pre match. Another classic that was often thrown out at us "no second fiddle" I have heard how they start the orchestra with the first violin so I always figured no second fiddle meant exactly that, be first, WIN! Be first to each ball, be first to every tackle, do not allow your opponent to beat you at any stage of the game. These were for sure great lessons to be learning, who would have wanted a group of young kids playing sports to think anything less? Be determined and win, a simple message really yet for me it sunk in deeper and became a little distorted. Maybe not distorted but the idea of who exactly was my opponent, this is where the distortion started, on any match day well who was the opponent, the other team obviously. The boy whom I am marking for the duration of the game is the one I must beat, I must beat him in every tackle and be first to the ball every time it is played into the area where we are positioned. Sounds simple enough, the distortion for me was never around a field of play or game day Sunday, I was more confused about who had become my opponent, were all that wished me harm my opponent or even those who possessed any kind of simple threat to me, my friends or my family or even worse, to my money. So in theory and to the best of all of my knowledge these kinds of threats were "the" opposition and I must not let them win.

I did not look any deeper or try to decipher any multitude of angles of who is my opponent is or was, anybody who looked to tell me what to do represented themselves to my mind as opposition. So what would any young boy do in these situations where he was met with opposition? Of course, you guessed it, no second fiddle. Does that mean when I heard my sports coach tell me to not let another player dictate to me how the game should be played, somewhere in my mind I only understood it to mean do not let anybody tell me what to do. A winning determination had been born inside of me that to this day and this very moment I am not sure if I can let it go. It definitely is beginning to take shape now that a bunch of teenage years of never listening to anyone and not letting anyone tell me what to do has now brought about the lock and key that I now sit behind. When you don't let society tell you what to do and continue to do whatever you want, then society might just turn around and say "bold boy, you cannot just do whatever you want when it leads to breaking the law. Lock him up"

So who really becomes the opposition then? Society and all authority within it or just those who are directly involved in making the rules of how you should live your life, the local cops who now know you too well. I would have to think it is never a good idea to be known by your local law enforcement, well not too well known at least. There are the teachers from school who want to guide a young person in how they should act and live, your own parents who have your best interests close to their heart and there is always the odd neighbour or two, a close friend's parents will have their advice for you from time to time too. Maybe it is time to give these people a little deeper looking in to.

THE COPS

Mr. Policeman, do you think it would serve our whole community better if you just did actual police work, do they know that a group of teenagers chatting is not some serious criminal event. Would it be possible to not start driving slowly by me as I walk home on a dark evening, your intimidation tactics work only to form a hatred of you. Just because I am younger does not mean you can be disrespectful to me for absolutely no reason.

So we are young and we loiter, what else can teenagers do, it is almost like we are criminal for just meeting up with our friends and forming a group. I have to think that no parent wants eleven teens taking over their house, does any home have a kitchen big enough for a group of teenagers to hang out in? So we take to the streets where we can meet up with our friends and we will discuss anything from music and movies to the latest viral videos on hacks and jokes that are now trending. It is a time to bond with our peers, the innocent conversation flows between us as it is within this arena among our peers that our opinion means something. We are spending time hanging out doing nothing really, on the inside though we are developing our own voice, we are developing opinions and shaping ourselves into the adults we are about to become. The topic of conversation may have changed over the years as in, once upon a time the chat could have been about the weekend movie and did we see it or not, what did we think and what was our favourite part. A single movie that played on channel two once a week, we may have had a very long conversation about this on a get together of a Thursday night, just standing around in the cold. Is it so wrong to just allow young people to be young and "hang out" that is what we do, there is no harm in teenagers being in a group laughing and joking together. Nowadays it could be the same conversation without the single movie once a week from a single channel, today has way more channels and a lot more going on the internet but the teenage way to figure all this out is just show up and chat about it.

The only time we might ever see "Mr. Law man" use a notion of a pre-emptive nature is when dealing with a group of teens hanging around the streets on a dark winters evening. Will people employed to serve as peace keepers, yes the police that is, will they respond to a call of domestic violence and upon their arrival there is no commotion and there are no witnesses and no evidence or any signs of a physical altercation. Will they use their pre-emptive powers of judgment to hurry a woman and her children to safety for a "just in case" solution, probably not. Will the peace keepers who are employed to uphold the law, will they enter into a bar on a Saturday night and do a walk around to every person holding an alcoholic beverage in their hand and demand from them their car keys, probably not. Mind you would this not be a wonderful effort to pre-empt drunk driving or uphold the law of no driving under the influence of alcohol and most notably PREVENT a horrible traffic accident from occurring. This would be a good preventative measure to take. Will the police officers ever even learn the laws so that they might begin to turn away from the idea that a group of teenagers on the street means trouble and they must harass the youth, always of course only in a pre-emptive nature. Preventing any crime to occur because teenagers are just criminals by default. Such nonsense breeds a hatred within young people of the police and for absolutely no reason. Well harassment is a crime in itself that the police would be guilty of when dealing with the youths. Here is a tip for the police, how about getting involved with the young people from an early age and show yourself as a positive role model who might actually give a shit about the young people progressing in life and not always in the role of placing road blocks in their life when they reach their teenage years of "hang out" time.

Seventeen and Life

What did we do all through my younger years was just that, simply, hang out. Walk out of our homes in the evenings and head down the road to hang out, sometimes there was a little coupling going on and a boyfriend and girlfriend got together for some innocent fun and in general we just walked from point A to point B and shared some extra laughs. Some would show up a little late and maybe even the conversation got repeated as they missed it earlier and some would head home early too. All in all 99% of the time there was no breaking the law going on. However when the police see a group of young people hanging out of any random evening, they must harass 100% of the time. I have actually seen a charge sheet from the police to a teenager that read "his demeanour looked like he would cause trouble later that night"

I was sixteen and on a Saturday night out with two friends. My friends were a little older than me and were of legal age to be drinking alcohol and enjoying themselves in the bars, I on the other hand was legally too young although I had been getting away with it for some years now, I was too young.

Towards the end of the night the three of us were walking up the street heading towards one of my friend's homes, as we came to an intersection of the streets which lies at a curve along the street we were walking on, we noticed two cop cars sitting parallel parked in darkness. One of my friends remarked immediately "oh fuck, the cops" I remember saying, say nothing just keep walking.

It was really weird to see the cops just sitting parked like that. My friends reaction says it all really, why should someone fear the cops, definitely a "wrong" within society and youth.

We crossed through the intersection and upon reaching the opposite side we could hear the cops cars starting up. We continued our chatting as we walked and did not turn back to see what the police were doing. The cars revved loudly and sped off from their parked position and very quickly were pulling in to the side of the street directly behind us. I turned my head to see, well I swung my body around to see and just like that as quick as I had turned around the cop that was driving the first car was already out of the car and walking towards me. I knew him by his name and before I could speak it I was met with a full force punch to my face, as I was completely unaware this was what was coming and in the two or three seconds I had to see prior to receiving the punch I did see there were four cops per car and they were all getting out in a bit of a hurry.

As I went back a little from the punch I was asking "what the Fu...." another punch is landed to the back of my head from one of the other cops. Right at the point on the street where this is happening there is a little alleyway that leads to the backs of the houses and is a little short cut to another street, I was being pushed and punched into this alleyway. I was receiving a beating from the police, no provoking and

Seventeen and Life

definitely no advance warnings just five or six cops all swinging for me and my head. I can tell you that when a bunch of people jump on you and start beating you, well let's just say the confusion level is quite intense. On this particular night confusions were what the fuck are they doing but the mind needed to concentrate hard and very quickly. When in fights in the streets previously or in a bar fight, I have been involved in one or two, anyway I have found my own strategies to fighting and the simplest way to explain it would be like this, if you can see what is coming your way then you have some milliseconds to be prepared for the blow you are about to receive, this will allow you to make tense the area and the hit doesn't hurt so much really. But on this night the hits were coming from, I didn't even know where, blow after blow. Fists punching me and then hard cracks of batons, you know the things some people call them night sticks. I was against a wall of the alleyway and beaten to the ground, at this point I had no choice but to curl up as best I could and bring my arms up around my head, one of the scumbag cops kept pulling on my arm trying to get a clear shot at my head. I had my body curled up, my knees tucked up tight to my elbows and my arms bent up with hands locked together around the back of my head. They were now kicking and punching and the occasional blow from the night sticks really did hurt. I had tensed my entire body to endure the beating that I was getting and it felt like an hour or more but in real time it was probably about ten minutes.

What of my two friends I hear you ask, I learned the next day from them that they were both pushed up the street by two of the cops and they were threatened to be hit with the night sticks too. I heard from them that following day, they had let me know there were five of them or possibly six cops beating on me in the alleyway. My friend told me they saw all the cops beating on me but there was nothing they could do.

As I was lying there all tensed up, the beating finally stopped and as quickly as they had all jumped out of the squad cars, they were running off and jumping back into them. I had an angle of view of the pavement only as my face was flat to the ground and all that I could see was about five or six inches above it, their uniform shoes was all that I could see as they quick stepped away. I wanted to make sure that they had all made their getaway and I was safe to get back up to my feet. I was sore all over, my muscles were almost cramp like from all the tensing I had been doing during the awful walloping I had just received. I stood up and looked around, my two friends were no longer there and so I headed up the street towards home. Not even one hundred yards along that street and a cop car had sped up beside me and from it jumped out two policemen, only two policemen this time. My walk was that of a very sore person, half on the ball of my foot on one leg and the bare heel of the other. My shoulders were lowered and stretched which caused my head to hang low, this was about the most comfortable I could make my body as I walked along the street.

When I turned to see the two cops out of the car and coming towards me all that I could think was, here we go again, Fuck it!. They did not come upon me to throw any punches and I was not met with any kicks, no instead it was a pair of handcuffs and verbal cautioning of the fact that I was being arrested and detained under a breach of the peace law. So really my night had gone so far and just to keep things clear, from walking up the street with two friends to being jumped by a handful of on duty cops, left in alleyway to figure it out and then arrested for breaking some sort of peace or other. The hand cuffs had been placed on me and I was thrown into the back of the cop car. One cop jumped in the front to drive and the other in the back with me and en route to the local cop station, the fool sitting in the back with me threw his elbow into my gut a few times. By this time I had had enough of it, my thoughts you might wonder? "Fuck those cops and their bully tactics" & "if I am to be done for a breach of the peace, Fuck it I might as well start a breaching" I mean come on man I may only be a teenager, but I know the difference that the charge I am being arrested under is bogus and a beat down that I had received that night just cannot be legal. Being a teenager just makes me wrong by default, what can a youngster do about that?   I started to verbally abuse the coppers in the car, I directed the most of it at the one driving and every time I got a good deep sly dig in verbally I received from the cop in the back a severe blow of his elbow to my stomach. When we arrived to the cop station and just as I was hauled out of the back of the car and to my feet, nearly simultaneously the driver had jumped out and ran around and delivered to me a full force kick up in the ass. It was one of those real life "broke his foot off In my ass" kicks. When we entered the police station, I was escorted in my handcuffs and the desk man who was ready to take my details had pushed the door buzzer to allow us walk through to an office area bypassing the front desk reception area. I was asked "for the record please state your name" and due to the tone that had been set for the evening, me being beaten around for no good reason and my only option of a response was to hurl more insults and verbal abuse, so I replied "go fuck yourself". I will admit, this was kind of lame but it was all I had. After my beating that evening and the continued elbows to my stomach, I was lucky to be able to even answer back at all. Of course my reply was not received too well and a rap of policeman's knuckles across the back of my head was as good as the policeman standing behind me had got for me. That particular copper had been twisting the handcuffs and making it as unpleasant and sore from the very first moment after my bonus "boot in the hole" when we had arrived.

The desk sergeant did not have any appreciation for the smack to my head that the arresting officer had delivered and he immediately chastised the officer. The desk sergeant was an older man and seemed to have a much more placid demeanour, with that he ordered the officer to release me from my handcuffs and I really didn't know exactly what to think. My immediate thought was maybe I am just going to be let go home, a second thought was "Fuck these cops, all three of them" so the officer began to undo the shackles from my wrists. Back to my thoughts right then though, I mean seriously? Where does it state or is it written that just because I had about twenty thoughts in twenty seconds, where does it mean that I am a problem child or some kind of teenager that deserves special attention. Being accused of being too smart and too quick with my brain like it was a negative aspect of my character, I think the adults of my younger years should probably have tried to nurture this along rather than belittle me and put me down for it, have you ever heard such a ridiculous statement as "too smart for his own good" what a stupid thing to even say. But I got accused and heard this kind of thing a lot.

I continued to throw a bit of abusive language at the cops and the one standing to my right was taking the bait every time. The desk sergeant spoke to him firmly again repeating his position on "how we treat people" all people. The one officer behind my back had given a little squeeze on the cuffs, his sly way to hurt me one last time. Think about it though, for the past three hours these guys have been beating up on me at random and for no good reason either so of course I am thinking as sharp as I can although I will admit with all the aching around my entire body it was really hard to get my mind clear and away from the hatred for the cops right then and there.

Fuck these fucking assholes was repeating in my brain, the officer removed my left hand first and then the right, I took a sigh and then within possibly a millisecond I swung for the cop to my right and did catch him totally unaware, the cop behind me was fumbling with the handcuffs as he was putting them away, I knew it was my ideal opportunity and for all of the beating that I had received that night, this was my chance to do a little beating of my own. The cop had fallen back from my punch and I lunged at him quickly to land another blow before he could scramble up to his feet from the desk where he was sprawled across. He grabbed for me and I grabbed a hold of him and we began circling the floor, when the second cop had jumped on my back we moved across another desk and not only did papers fly from it but a typewriter or computer also crashed to the floor. I swung and kicked a little more for the guy on my back and we bounced off of a filing cabinet, knocking it over too. The desk sergeant was roaring at us to stop but it was just mayhem really. Chairs were scratching across the floor as we bumped into them and a half filled coffee cup spilled across a bunch of paperwork while another crashed off the floor. I found myself wrestled down to the ground by the three of them and to be honest I knew that I did not have much of a chance anyway but after the beating I had taken that evening earlier, I needed to give it a go.

The funny thing about the charges against me and my day in court following that particular night, there was no mention of broken office equipment or the assault on the officers inside of the police station. And to be honest about it the charges that did follow on could not have been any more absurd.

My charge sheet read;

1. BREACH OF THE PEACE

2. Assault of a police officer (from the incident in the alleyway)

3. Threats to the life of a police officer.

4. Drunk and disorderly in public.

5. Actual bodily harm to a police officer.

All of those charges for a sixteen year old who was just walking up a street with his friends and somehow I got all these charges as their "pre-emptive measure" (to save from me trying to sue them). My friends were visited by the police and warned that should they think about giving any evidence or witness testimony on my behalf, they would be receiving their own charge sheets and be dragged into the court system also. I am fully aware that you may be thinking right about now that there must be other parts to this incident or it cannot be true and all I can say to you is, that is how it happened and even on my day in court when I was called to the stand to answer the charges that had been brought against me, I replied

"Not guilty your Honour, not guilty."

When the prosecutor asked me about "the night in question" and they do have a very sly way of asking too, "when you were in the action of assaulting the police officer, you also made threats to slit his throat and a promise to kill him. Isn't this true mister Mc Nally?"

I really had no clue how to answer this question, not only had he tried to make me say yes or no to the threats part of the question but in doing so would be like I was confirming the piece about being "in the act of assault", like is it not bad enough that an entire night/evening shift of police officers were willing to beat up a teenager, lie about it to their superiors so as to bring about false criminal charges against that very same teenager, to follow it all the way through the legal system and continue the lies all along the journey and to give false evidence in the courtroom to a judge. It does seem far fetched when I read back over this and to expect you to believe it. Well it is indeed how it all happened and so my response to the public prosecutor,

"I did not assault the policeman nor did I make any threats to his life"

The superintendent was not happy with my answer and asked again with a lead up statement, "we know you assaulted the officer in question and isn't it true that you threatened to slit his throat to kill him?"

Again I was shocked at what I was hearing, I raised my arms up as I began answering

"I did not threaten anybody's lives and it was impossible for me to assault anybody while I had my head very tightly between my hands and arms like this so as to protect myself from the severe beating I was receiving from the officers in question and a few more of them, I was the one being assaulted"

I was sitting in the witness stand of the courtroom and I was facing the judge with my arms bent up across my ears and my hands clutched together behind the back of my head. I spoke directly to the judge and asked him how on earth could it be possible to assault anyone from this position?

The judge could not look at me directly to my face and as he turned his head to look down to his desk and his papers he had a nod and a wink to the policeman who happened to be the public prosecutor also, within seconds I was dismissed from the witness stand. This was justice, this was the system I was growing up in and expected to respect. Please, give me a break! I am not sharing this with you to expose poor, well let's face it, piss poor policemen and an absolutely disgraceful system. I am sharing with you to hopefully shed a little light on how it can be for a young man. Many teenagers are guilty of nothing other than being too young to understand any difference between abuse of power by the cops and their own rights as a human being.

Seventeen and Life

Being a teenager in trouble with the law can be something that can happen really easily, it is not always the child's fault. The cops who drive around at night meddling with teenagers perhaps should be questioned about their own motives too. How easy it can be for a few police officers to screw up a young man's life. So all of a sudden the youth says "fuck the police". It is not right nor has it been right within my own life, but hey these are just some of the problems facing a teenager as they try to get through. And to finish about the rant on cops, think about it, what sort of government employees take pleasure in intimidating young adults?

Oh yeah! what about teachers too?

SCHOOL IS GREAT.

School was another epic time of becoming a teen, the development stages of life. I know we touched on them a little earlier but it is worth giving some thought to what exactly is going on in teenage years. I am reflecting back to try and find or piece it all together and hope to gain clues to the why and the how and all of that.

Remember I am sitting in a prison cell wondering how in the fuck did I ended up here. You on the other hand are hopefully snuggled up on the couch with your shoes off and maybe even some kind of drink beside you having a good read about my life. Coffee or tea or maybe even hot chocolate, I wasn't thinking of wine or brandy by the way.

There is nothing worse than being late to wake up for school, while it is not the class or subject you are worried about. No, more like the smell of your arm pits and being a teenager now, it can sometimes be from your groin too. So what is a better method? Be late for school because you needed to shower? Or be just about on time for school but have a smell of body odour off you the entire day?

A self consciousness that a young boy does not need to be dealing with and again no help from any of the adults who have gone before me. In this bigger school we have to sit beside girls and have partners in some classes for projects and that can mean moving around close to people. At least in my junior school years I could sit in the one seat all day long and move very little even though there was less of a smell off me ever in those early years. Smelling right only brought about a new way of being self conscious and a little rattle to the foundations of self confidence that I had always just thought was naturally formed. I didn't want to know that I might have to sit and hope nobody could smell any part of me at all. I wasn't sure if the teachers that came into class smelling of b.o, did they do it to make some of us more comfortable (those of us being teenagers who were already self conscious about odours) or were they just despicable people in their own lives. Who really knows, my excuse for smelling like crotch from time to time was my body experiencing some hormonal changes due to my age, the teachers excuse on the other hand? I cannot even begin to imagine what their excuse is or was, oh god no, this just made me think that there might still actually be still some smelly teachers teaching the children of today, gross!

What is the job of a teacher? To be a lesson giver by way of text book and academic learning. Yeah sounds great but what about all the other stuff like setting an example to the new young adults to be. What of being a role model to the pupils that sit before them every morning, girls all freaked out because their periods are throwing them into major cyclones of despair born out of embarrassment as they have not found a comfort level yet in their life to be able to stand and walk to the bathroom to handle their tampon business. A blushing red faced girl tries to hide something in her sleeve as she starts for the door while speaking to the teacher in a quite mumble about going to the toilets. Boys who have not showered in the morning before school and stink nastily from the most enjoyable wet dream the night before. More simply stinking from playing a game of soccer at their break time finding their school uniform shirt has stuck to them from sweating armpits. How lovely the crowd of us young students were to sit in front of you teacher, we have our excuses of being young. We are unknowing what it is to be an adult and how to take care properly of our personal hygiene as we are only beginning on our journey of puberty. Yes we are young and again too young and innocent to understand why you the teacher come into our classroom stinking like you have played in our soccer game or you decided not to shower in the morning before heading or to work....... What was your excuse for smelling?

Work! Yes work, you are being paid a salary to stand In front of us young teenagers and teach us. Teaching, they used to say was a vocation in life and teachers do it for the love of the job. The salary is secondary to a teacher as their satisfaction lies in producing high marks from achieving brats. Nah seriously they wish to help in the education of the young and work tirelessly to achieve such feats as to be a part of the development of a young person into a well rounded and educated human being.

I can clearly remember thinking to myself and most definitely not out loud "why is this teacher stinking so bad, please do not come and stand even close to my desk or lean over me to correct anything in my copy books" so where really is the role model position of the teacher in our young lives and to what extent is that shaping us for the future? We are born to our parents and outside of family friends the first outsider adults we encounter are our teachers, the people who can mould us as they wish and definitely as they are only human too they can only work within their own personal limitations of what life is about and what being a stand up person or human is all about to them, is what we will learn. Should a teacher be limited in their life skills or as I was saying earlier their own personal hygiene then this is what we can learn from them. Maybe parents should get to meet all the teachers prior to sending a child to a school and if something is not right then they could request that the teacher be made wash themselves on a regular basis and you know what? If you went to a school where there were no smelly teachers, you got a very lucky time in school. Those of us who had smelly teachers had to just suffer in silence.

Drama is a much bigger part of it though and whether they smell or not would have nothing to do with it, the addiction to drama is something that seems just so huge in all walks of life and I suppose is unavoidable in the school rooms either. What can be meant by drama at school, no not the drama class or anything like that, more like the meddling teachers who want to pry and somehow justify their meddling under the fake idea of concern and righteousness. I have to imagine that people who love to pry and develop drama in any situation really just have a lot of issues going on for themselves. Could it be that in school having a teacher who stinks regularly and lives to create drama would be possibly the worst teacher of all? Yeah that is indeed a horrible combination alright, so us as children have little say in where we are going to go to school and just end up with some not so well adjusted teachers. Our choice has been what subjects we might like to learn and we made no choice to select our teachers and these will now become our influencers. If you are a parent and you visit the school your now teenager is about to attend next year and you meet the teachers and one of them stinks, it is definitely allowed to bring this up. There is no room for trying to avoid it because you do not wish to offend them, how else will it ever change? And this psychology that if you mention it means there is something wrong with you and you are the one that likes drama, well stop and think for a moment and know full sure that you are doing a civic duty in not allowing it to be twisted back on you and continue with your complaint as there is no excuse for a role model or an influencer of your children not to have the basic skills of personal hygiene and the "drama" we could do without. Of course it is necessary for some teacher appreciation to be on the look out for any signs of abuse in children and hopefully can continue to detect problems in students and be the voice that can reach a young person who may be suffering but prying and meddling with children is a drama class that has no place in the school

I went out one evening with some friends and we did a little drinking in a field before heading to the pub for some more beer, only in the pub it is a little more refined and the beer comes in a nice pint sized glass, more expensive though but a nicer and much warmer atmosphere too. It was a Sunday afternoon and in the autumn and winter months in Ireland it can be quite cold outside and so to be out drinking in the fields isn't a very good way to spend the night. What a great idea to head for the pub and enjoy the open fire and the all round heat of the place. I used to meet up with this older crowd and did my drinking with them as I was only thirteen and if they knew my real age I would say that would have been the end of their friendships and help in getting me drink. I would say they all thought I was seventeen and just under the age by a little bit so what harm for them to buy pints for me as I was close to legal age anyways. Little did they know how young I really was.

It was legal to smoke in the bars back then and we would take up our spot in the pool room of the bar on a Sunday evening and enjoy a few cigarettes along with the cool pints of beer and the heat of the bar of course which was the big bonus. We would play some games or pool enjoying the songs from a juke box and plenty of laughs and jokes. Most of the laughs and jokes came by way of slagging each other off about something or other and maybe even the full run down on who was shifting who on Saturday night. Basically a fun time and a lot of laughs. Thinking back to those Sundays brings a smile to my mind as they were fun even though they have to rank about as devilish as could be, me at only thirteen years of age, smoking and drinking in a bar on a Sunday evening, so of course I liked them evenings, I was only breaking all kinds of laws by just my presence alone. But again I was big kid so I was not far off the size of these older guys and so I didn't look out of place, I could shoot pool pretty well too so I held my own on the table and when it came to drinking I liked that too and I could hold my own with sucking down pints too.

They night was coming to an end in the pub and closing time was upon us, last orders or last drinks were being called by the barman and it was the mark of the end to the night. Most of the lads and girls in my company had work or college the following Monday morning and so there would be no back to anyone's house after this, only head on out and get the bus home. The pub we were in has a front bar and a back bar and then the pool room as well, this is where we were. There is a long hallway from the front to the back and the hallway runs along the side of the front bar so you didn't really go into or through the front bar to walk through to the back bar which you had to walk through to go the pool room. The hallway to the back was long yes well, longish let's just say and was narrow. When it came time to leave we were heading out and

Seventeen and Life

I was the last one or our crew leaving for the night and as I got to the front door which was now closed over because closing time was upon us so as I came to the door I had to close it behind me as I exited. When I came to the door there were people also exiting from the front bar of the pub and so they were in the hallway just behind me, I turned to see and had to hold the front door open for them as they were leaving also. If I did not hold the door open it would have been one of those real rude situations like slamming a door in someone's face and so I held my hand on the door for the next person coming out to hold it for the next, by the time the first of them from the front bar got the door about three others were in the hallway exiting also and lone behold it was a gathering of teachers from my new secondary school.

Sunday evening and out for a few pints were the teachers, who was I to judge? I didn't have any of the teachers for any classes from the ones I could see and I just knew it was the vice principal of the school and a metal work teacher from the school and the third in the hallway one of the math teachers but not the one that I had for math. The vice principal thanked me for holding the door as he reached for it and I continued on out and over for my bus.

I did not give any of that evening too much thought and it had been another good night out with my friends. Just another Sunday evening and nice few beers were had, a real lovely jubly kind of evening.

On Monday morning I headed to school and sat in for the first few classes and did my usual exit routine right around eleven a.m. break time. There were three classes in the morning to where I was there having been dropped off by my parents on their way to work. First break was around eleven o'clock and that would give me my first chance of escape. Naturally I took the escape chance most mornings and I was gone. I would walk through the fields or along the railway tracks back to my home so that nobody would see me or notice that I was ducking off of school for the day. Once home and the school uniform was taken off, well then it was okay to be seen around the streets or wherever because in that school uniform you could be hauled off right back to school by almost anyone. The uniform was like a beacon for "kid mitching school" and anyone around the area would be taking notice if a child walking the streets or the road home in their uniform at only eleven in the morning. Lunchtime it is expected to see school kids down through the town but not that hour or earlier. There were mornings I would have ducked out from school and made a beeline for the bus stop hoping to escape with ease and no one would see me, I may have meant to be out from school on my way home or to an appointment, who would really know? Best not take any chances was my normal routine of mitching and stick to the fields and the railway tracks were always the safer route. It would be no good to be passed by the police wearing your school uniform at that hour of the morning and get quizzed by them or even brought back to the school and delivered directly to the principal's office. So the railway tracks were always a much safer route, as far as not to be seen by any of the authorities or even a teacher on their way in to school for later classes.

On the Tuesday of that particular week I was walking through the corridor of school making my way from one class to the next and when I arrived at my class my year head teacher was by the door, I could see her standing there and I knew it was not geography class so why was she there? All the other kids were now heading the same way along the corridor and we had a one way system in place along the corridors so there was no turning back. My history teacher and my year head were both standing at the door to the class room and to me, yes I had history class but this year head standing there spelled trouble. I had seen them make a quick "look away" when they saw me turning the corner, almost like I could read their lips "here he comes now". No turning back for me against the stampede of other students heading to class and so fuck it, here we go. What do they..... want? Could you follow me to my office she says and it wasn't in any kind of mean or hateful tone or anything, almost like I was not in trouble but needed to go for some routine standard questionnaire or something. I followed her along the halls and as all the other students were now in classes the hallways had gone super quiet. I did not even really know this teacher at all and definitely did not know she had an office or where it even was. She unlocked a door down by the main canteen area and invited me in, I made a bit of an awkward gesture to the seat in the room and she gave a nod of approval to me taking the seat. She began with a counsellor slash therapist type of approach, "now Aidan how much alcohol do you consume?" I immediately thought, ah hear what the fuck is this and who does she think she is with her fake concern. She had a note pad and pen at the ready for my answer and I really was not too worried about any kind of a trap or whether I should answer honestly or lie a little, ah what's the difference. "I have a few pints on the weekends usually" simplest answer I could think of really. Her dropping the pen was a bit of a giveaway to her disapproval of my reply I suppose. She composed herself and asked the next question "is that every weekend or just a Saturday night every so often?" At this stage in my young teenage years and so early in life I really had no patience for this kind of prying session with a figure head and I had built up enough sarcasm and pure cheek that you may guess how the rest of that interview goes. I started to answer back alright but I wanted to save her all the long drawn out nonsense so I let her have it.

"listen miss, what is it you want to know? Am I drinking? Yes I am and I have been for quite some time now. I drink on weekends and on school nights if so happens to be a session, I might drink a couple of litres of cider and or seven or eight pints in the pub, it all really depends on what is going on. I don't see what the big investigation is about and I would appreciate if you can just stop trying to pry into my life. I do good with my grades and as a teacher isn't that all you should be concerned about?"

Yup that had her gasping for breath alright, she had no clue I or any student could be so straight out and cheeky as it just wasn't the way a pupil spoke to a teacher in them days at least. She went on to quiz me about how did I think a young man of thirteen years of age could think it was alright to be using alcohol and of course she kept going back to "what will your parents think". To me it was just another boring lecture from someone who was old and well I suppose I saw her as more than old, she was ancient in my eyes and just being nosey and annoying for no real or obvious reason. She had not given me any indication of a clear reason behind her questioning and her lecture. I just flat out in the middle of her talking decided I had heard enough and wanted to be on my way. "Can I go now or what?" She stopped mid speech and told me I could go when she was finished and I needed to hear what she had to say to which my very simple and clear reply "I do not need to hear anything you have to say, I will be on my way now and if you are just trying to make trouble for me then you should question your own motives" then she had a go off my attendance in school and that it is clear that I have a drinking problem, to that I stood up and said goodbye, this conversation is over and out from her office I walked and on out the front doors and followed along my usual route of heading home early.

School was just boring to me and it did come easy all the academics and all but there was no spark to keep me there. I was too young to fully express my thoughts correctly and ask teachers to find a way to make it more interesting. Within a week or two of my meeting with the year head I was called to the principal's office for a similar line of questioning, my year head teacher was standing in her office also and the nun who was head of the school was telling me she will be ringing my parents to come and collect me and explaining to them all about my drinking and my lack of attendance in school. I answered her with a rebellious tone and attitude and kindly asked her to go F herself, I was not intending to be coming back and I walked out the front door and down the steps.

What I was unaware of was that my father had received phone calls about this meeting and the meeting with the year head teacher from the first time she had asked me questions. My father was not too pleased to be receiving such and let me know how it was not the fact that she had called him to discuss me and my drinking but her questions followed on to my father and to pry into how much drinking does my father do and to what extent was there unrest within the homestead. Her tone with him was somewhat disgusting towards him is how he had explained it to me, even though I was not out of hot water for the drinking that I was doing but my dad had made very clear to me that he was very pissed off at the cheek and nerve of a teacher to call him to question him. My dad explained to me what he had expressed to the teacher "why don't you concentrate on the teaching and let him worry about what his son does on weekends" and how he runs his household. Furthermore he did explain how he took immediate issue with the teacher over the phone over the fact that I had rarely been to school lately and perhaps if more time was spent figuring out a way to keep me stimulated, perhaps even some ground breaking teaching techniques, maybe Aidan might stick around in school a bit more often. So the teacher had called my dad to pry and make an attempt to meddle in his family and the home life of mine only to be met with the criticisms my father had for the teaching methods and skills whereas I could not be kept within school for any length of time due to the inability of the teachers to raise their efforts to the level that I had needed.

And so after some very severe telling offs and talking's to, I was pretty much done with what teachers had to say or do in my life either.

So there I had learned in a simple review of my time as a younger teenager I have had the major role models and I suppose ground breaking folks in a young man's life, shattered. The teachers, I had learned by thirteen could do more mischievous meddling than teach. I know it can be the lifeline that may help someone in a very real abusive situation in their home life to find and help a student who may be suffering but shouldn't there be some kind of program to teach the teachers to know the difference, maybe spot a student who is too bored by the basic academics and not assume the problem is at home.

And the good old law keepers or as I understand them, keepers of the peace. By sixteen my understanding was to never trust a law man, never let your guard down when dealing with a police officer. Most importantly that they can and will lie just to screw your life up. They love the drama and for some reason seem to be thought to keep an overactive suspicious mind and consider themselves as untouchable as they seem to have a crossover in their brains that "they are the law" instead of an understanding that they are to uphold the law and are just humans same as me or you. After the beatings I had taken and a number of fake and false charges brought against me, well seriously, who could respect these people. Why not have a program of education for them as well to gain understanding and recognise their own wrong doings and have their aim not to suspect every person they encounter but more like work with the public, get in the community and become a role model. A position of someone within the community who could be trusted to actually do good as opposed to the position they take of trying to be intimidating to lay folk.

At only sixteen years of age and I could understand that quite clearly already. Does this make me mistaken or right? Hard to know sometimes or do most of you out there just not give these things any consideration at all? I guess it takes a lot of people to want to change a society to become concerned enough to actually begin about change within certain systems.

HOW SILLY.

I have always enjoyed hanging out with friends and sharing laughs, I mean it is what we do as kids and children growing up. I wanted to take a moment and cruise through some ideas with you and about really how I have learned some things and completely had no clue of others.

I never thought when I was just a child racing little wooden sticks as boats in the streams that I one day would grow up. I enjoyed my playing for sure but I had no idea that one day I would be bigger and have more responsibility. It absolutely never crossed my mind. If you think back to when you had a nice happy feeling as a child, do you ever relive that feeling or has it gone forever as you grow up? Of course we are not supposed to even know stress as a child and why would we stress over the future and what it will all be like when we grow up. Then as we move into our teenage years things just start changing. Somehow a switch is turned on to begin our journey of stress, we do not know what exactly to stress about and so we begin creating a little here and there. If you are like me you might not worry about how school exams go but you may worry as to who might laugh at you.

Seventeen and Life

If our hair is not right or our laces are not right, there are too many things to worry about in our small world as our teen years get underway. How do I look has had its importance over the years and definitely we all know the cliché of having acne, greasy spotty face and for a time in the morning In front of the mirror it can seem like the world has come to an end because of our greasy little new inhabitants on our face. The funny thing about the acne is that somehow it is almost like our peers and the closer friends of ours do not even bat an eyelid at our new growth, it is as if everyone just understands that we all get them and it is no big deal, so what was the stressing for? Worth a thought isn't it, that a lot of stuff we may believe to be oh so important and devastating to our lives might just be some normal piece of life that nobody even cares about.

The body odour, well as I mentioned earlier it can cause a great amount of being self conscious as well. Not everyone can smell it off you and when someone does and they mention or make any reference to it out loud in public, now there is a situation where it would be nice if the ground opened up and swallowed you, for sure. But again it is still something that can happen for all of us in our teenage years and it just takes a little getting used to and of course we are just learning about personal hygiene. I am aware it can be different for girls than boys and I can only recall my early teenage years as a boy. I do recall on the odd occasion getting some bad smells off some girls though and I never once ever spoke of it and definitely would not say it out loud in front of anybody. I just felt a little sorry for the girl but figured that because their bodies go through a lot more changes than ours with multitudes of different chemicals running around their system that maybe from time to time they get to smell worse than us too. I will admit I was innocent enough to think that girls were made of sugar and spice and all things nice and so I expected a sweet bubble gum flavour scent from them all of the time. Like I never thought a girl might smell like I do or have smelly feet when they take their socks off. But I grew up with all brothers and so never had a sister to experience at first hand what the smelly side of a girl might even be. I really did think that a girl was like perfume or a flower and smelled nice all of the time. Yet these are the little things we start to learn to stress over and we can begin to form little ways in which we handle and deal with things that come up for us in front of and between us and our peers.

Do we know as a teenager that it all probably doesn't really matter anyway? No not really, yet we are in a new era and our childhood days are behind us, responsibilities are being placed on us by friends and family, teachers and football coaches. We are gaining our own place in the world and did I ever think at any stage about growing up and becoming even older and moving into adulthood, nah not really. The same innocent me was happy enjoying the time in the here and now and looking for the next laugh to be had. I never knew what tomorrow might hold but the funny thing about that is I never cared and it didn't come into any equations of mine as to what might be next or where all of this is going.

Thoughts of how life is and what it is and who are we and where do we fit in, these are all genuine and possible new stress levels of a teenager that though may seem like nothing, can be brought to fully consume any person on any given day. The part about we are all the same and we are all made equal is another part of growing up that I learned is not really true. Some people may have to figure out their way across a crowded room and have to plan in their mind of exactly how to navigate through the assembly room of any school morning and what approach they will make and how to exit as they find their path in and around the mass or students that have gathered. Such a person may even have palms that begin to sweat at the thought of making the trip across the large hall type room. Such are nervous or stressing moments, though it may seem like nothing for a lot of people, it can be the absolute world to someone and having some understanding that even the simple items in our daily lives can be one hell of chore for another person can help that person maybe navigate their way across that hall room a little easier. It does not have to be mentioned or discussed but the new stress in a young person's life can be alleviated just the tiniest bit by walking with them or stepping aside when you see them approach.

As teenagers we seem to learn about these new things to stress about and find ways in convincing ourselves that nothing else matters and so we begin to learn about drama and mini dramas too. Some adults I know definitely carry this part of their early years all the way with them and still are living with the love for drama and others the dependency on their stress. Almost like they might not even know who they are them own selves if that element of who they are was ever to be taken away. Others stress about nothing and barely ever have too many thoughts about nothing much really and so do they have it any easier? I don't know really because I was always thinking. Probably stressing myself out over absolutely nothing if the truth be told. I really never gave too much thought to how I might walk into a crowded room or how I might navigate my way across one though I did learn to stress about other stuff. I figured it is normal and continued along my merry way. I do however recall many times where I got embarrassed and the hatred of the feeling it brought with it.

What is that and where does it come from? I could see others who were not affected the same as me when it came to being embarrassed and I often wondered why on earth did this embarrassment thing have such a grip of me, even from such a young age it had always been there. A feeling of heat that could really fill me up and some how by its nature like a never ending cycle. To be embarrassed about something and then feeling more embarrassed about people around me noticing I was embarrassed so it has always been a feeling that grew larger and larger all by its self. I cannot be sure if you, right now reading this can identify or have any one such feeling that feels like it consumes you or just filled you right up and sustains itself by the nature of itself like the way my being embarrassed has done. I have heard that depression can be like that, that it feeds off itself and keeps going and going in a cycle that is hard to get out of. For me my embarrassed feeling does not last for weeks or months like depression might but it could last for a few minutes only maybe like five or ten minutes. .

I for sure have avoided many things to hide away from the feeling of being embarrassed, I didn't or more like could not find a way to chat with girls that I liked because inside my mind I did not or could not figure out a way to deal with the embarrassed feeling and of course if I was going to blush up in the face and feel all hot around my collar how could I play it cool to chat up a girl? Weird isn't it? How a simple feeling could have such power over me to bring about where I would rather avoid something or deny myself all because I was afraid of a feeling. And there is another one so through some sort of sensitivity within myself I would not speak up for myself at times and allow others to just air out whatever they needed to say because I did not want to become embarrassed and so I had a fear of "it". Even writing this now reminds me of how powerful these feelings were. I was cheeky and growing further into my teens I did learn some ways to cope with the feeling that I feared the most. I became louder and told myself not to give in to it any more. Someone had told me when they were speaking one day to me about embarrassment and feelings that why would anyone be so super sensitive about any feeling and chances are that those around us are enjoying or enduring their own feelings so that would give them less time to be able to pay any attention to what I might be going through anyway.

I had become more outspoken and began to care less about what people thought of me and there is a chance I should confess to, a chance that I over compensated for it. From going from a young child of say ten years of age who gave too much thought about what someone might think if they saw me going red or caught me in an embarrassing time, to a teenager who began to be someone who gave less and less thought of what anybody thought and could not have cared less who was watching or who was judging me. I kind of got the idea of yeah! Who the hell could be bothered with how I am feeling anyway. What does it matter if I am feeling an emotion and someone notices, like what really could happen? Yup you guessed it, nothing could happen and there really was and still is nothing to fear about how we feel at any given moment of any given day. Another side to this would be that in the time it took me to learn these smaller things about what I was feeling it also took me some time to understand that it was not the same for everybody and even though we all have feelings and emotions not everyone feels the same or has thoughts about their own feelings the same either.

I can for certain say that I did not care about what people thought of me and many would say that when you stop caring about yourself is a time when you give up worrying what others think of you too. I would argue that I very much loved myself and was totally surrounded by a very fat ego but I just morphed into not giving too much time, thought or concern into what others thought. At the age of fifteen years old I had become very much a reckless youth who did not seem to have a care in the world and was now living a much different life to what would or could be called the "norm". I did not care too much anymore and I rarely became embarrassed about anything. It did not mean that my feelings were not there any more, I guess it just meant that through these years I found a way to cope with them or more like hide them away and keep my own feelings and emotions all inside of myself and very personal. What was the key to that? Maybe even the alcohol use because by this age I was living the life of a working man and an adult and no longer doing the everyday childish things. If I wanted to chat with a girl it was much easier after a few drinks and should anyone catch me in a moment saying or doing something silly well maybe a fight could break out or something where I would be louder and more dangerous rather than just a shy kid.

It brings about some food for thought for sure about how we feel and how we learn about our own personal selves as we grow through our teenage years. For some, it all just flows like clockwork and for some others emotions can be a complete mine field. How can we all be the same and understand each other if we do not have a clear understanding of ourselves. Can it be possible to know what someone else might actually feel about any given thing or whether or not do we even consider their feelings often enough?

DRINKING ALCOHOL

I did, in all my early years experiment and drinking alcohol was a huge piece of that experiment and I have shared a few of my excursions with you a little earlier. What my real question as I rifle back through the memories and thoughts about development and feelings as a young boy into teenage years is how did I become me? Was I always the same and how did I arrive in prison? It is easy to think, well that's simple just go and do some really law breaking stuff and prison is exactly where you will end up. It has not been that simple for me and I will openly admit that drinking alcohol probably has a major part to play in where I find myself sitting.

I loved the way as I was saying my feelings had changed and drinking gave me so much of the clichéd "Dutch courage" yes it is true that talking with girls and chatting them up became a whole lot easier when alcohol was involved, though I still remained relatively shy even with a belly full of booze. I loved feeling buzzed and giddy and excited and really to think about for a second longer I was completely buzzed and excited about nothing really, just buzzed from the booze. Excited to be high and excited to be moving on to something more fun and better would be how I would have thought. This new stuff alcohol was amazing, all you had to do was be able to stomach it to where you were not like vomiting all the time and then the messy laughing and joking could go on for as long as you could keep pouring more alcohol in. How cool is that and what is not to like about it?

I can recall and very honestly report to you that with every great night out and every buzzed up laugh and joke there were consequences and little things that did indeed creep into my life that began a journey to becoming a person that was willing to do anything, go anywhere and absolutely say anything to anybody without a second thought in my mind, why? Probably because I was stuffing my emotions and becoming an unruly punk teenager who had some brains and some brawn to bring to the table now and along with that came this acceptance to violence. Being violent now had its own place in my world and there was no shame in being violent or most definitely no embarrassment when it came to being in a pub brawl or any kind of altercation. Who was I becoming through my constant abuse of alcohol? What is this new world I have led myself in to and what has it done for me or how have I allowed myself to be paid back from the life and lifestyle I have been choosing to continue in?

Who have I become ?

Is this me, the real me? Or some warped part of my life that is only temporary or will it continue forever? From a child who never thought of tomorrow or the future and was as care free as ever to a guy sitting in a jail cell contemplating every little aspect of life, not only wondering about my future and where on earth am I heading but already at only seventeen reeling back through the years to see where it all went wrong. Some turn about in a tiny progressive say seven years. Many older folks will find it hard to believe that a young boy could from ten and eleven years of age consume enough alcohol to bring about major life changes and that it would be impossible to have had enough time on earth to go through so much by such a young age. I am writing this to you with hand on heart there is so much detail I could go in to that would keep me writing for decades. The simple truth of the matter is that I am that soldier and I have done it in such a short space of time that I cannot understand even how myself, other than I am living it and have the fortunate experience to relate back to you, or as some may say, the misfortune, how and ever I am here and it is all very real Indeed.

Prison doesn't scare me or any or the lunatics out there on the landings because they would just be another fight or another problem to solve, my real worry is how will I get out of here and how on earth will I figure out what exactly is going on with me. What drives me to such extremes that I can end up somewhere like this in the first place? What brings a nice young innocent boy to a place like this in a matter of only a few years? Did I ever think that by laughing and joking and having great nights out which includes plenty of laughs with the lads to get togethers with the girls and the occasional fight in the streets would all lead to a little cell? Nah absolutely not, then again like I keep reminding myself to ask you, do you know what tomorrow holds for you?

So being drunk had this almighty power to feel invincible, somewhere where nobody could bring me down and never even take away my elation. What is it in us that we want to find such a place in the first place? Do you have to be sad to want to get drunk? In our culture in Ireland we have alcohol for all the occasions and we know it so well that it is the oldest joke around, we drink to celebrate and be happy and then we drink to be miserable and console ourselves too. A birthday party in Ireland is a good booze up and what could be called a "great session" and a funeral is a get together of probably the same people where the common denominator is a ton of booze too. Drinking alcohol is definitely a part of the culture here in Ireland, so much so that there are many business deals done over a drink in a pub and to just make a plan with a friend and do some simple socializing, yes for sure that is done at the pub too. A first date could be about meeting in a pub for a few drinks and letting the edge off a bit so as to set a comfort zone for both people to ease into their drunk selves to try and sell their souls to each other. To watch the sporting events is the perfect reason for a guy to go and meet his friends and have a few pints of beer and hang out with the lads. I saw these opportunities early on and had no problems at all finding a reason to be loading up on cans of beer or heading to the pub for pints. Nobody knew my real age and I had been in and out of the pubs for a number of years already by the time I was fifteen or sixteen it was believed that I was closer to twenty than I was to fifteen. If we were in America and we were asked for I.D. to just even enter a bar I would have been screwed but I still would have gotten alcohol somewhere anyway.

I found myself enjoying the social Saturday night in the pub and then the session afterwards either in someone's house or on the beach. We had loads of places to go drinking, the place I come from is a small fishing village where there are a number of fishing boats tied up on the weekends and various week nights that we always had somewhere to go and be indoors and out of sight to continue on drinking. If there was a session on somewhere then I wanted to be at it and getting more and more drink into me because this is what I did and there was not much time for anything else. But the war stories and the how it all happened is only one aspect of what drinking and alcohol meant in my life, it is time to look deeper into the emotional well being of myself and some of the how's and what not's that this, alcohol frenzy that I stirred myself in to, what's causing me to feel or not feel as the case may be.

Yes alcohol is promoted in an attractive way and so it can be easily said that falling into a trap of consuming anything is easy when the company's advertising efforts are multi-million dollar and have no discretion towards whether or not a young person is seeing these all the time. It can easily be said that the vibrant colours and all the smiling and laughing that goes on in such adverts gets deep into the psyche of a young man and so it holds a massive attraction from very early on. Again, Ireland has a drink culture and with many social gatherings always centred around the pub it is easy to grow as a young boy to teenager and want to be just like the older men in the pub. There is another element that is difficult to determine whether it is or has much to do with it but just like learning to drive a car, these are things that require an age limit to get a license and just like the pub there is an age limit to being able to buy alcohol and drink in the pub. Most young guys, of course not all, want to learn how to drive and be able to get a license and many want to be old enough to order their own pints of beer too. Maybe a yearning to be older has something to do with it. Being a teenager and feeling you have freedom is all taken away quite swiftly when you hit restrictions due to your age. It makes sense that there is an age limit as in reflecting back on my own life it does harden the case for the point to be made that a younger person has a much harder time handling alcohol and the effects and side effects brought about by alcohol use and or abuse. I guess it is deemed that it you are old enough to drink and be served legally in a pub then you would also be old enough to make reasonable decisions and choices and less likely to abuse the substance. It also makes sense that keeping something so powerful as alcohol away from teenagers as they are only developing and learning their own skill sets that why blur it all up with alcohol. Although some of the mainland Europe countries have a different view of alcohol and serve table wine with dinner where kids are allowed to consume the alcohol. It seems to be that our

European counter parts gain a respect for alcohol at a much younger age and the social problems attached to alcohol consumption appear less in such countries. Maybe they have been on to something very smart for many years now. They are also wine producing countries and wine is viewed much differently than here in Ireland. Our alcohol productions are more to yes a line of beers and strong beers too but the one true head banger stuff has to be the age old production of whiskey. I cannot ever imagine that it will become okay in Ireland for whiskey to be served to young people around the dinner table in the hope they will gain a respect for it and grow naturally with the same respect for the alcohol. Wouldn't you agree it would be fair to say that just because they are producers of wine would not be a factor in the gaining respect for alcohol but more their liberal attitude to alcohol, perhaps?

I drank alcohol to get buzzed and get high, there are no two ways about saying it. Alcohol gave me a different viewpoint and a much different platform to voice my opinions, I guess you could say the inhibitions were definitely lowered and this has to be a key to the full attractiveness that alcohol held for me. A young man who when wasted still laughed and giggled but now had all kinds of warped versions of reality and found the smallest stupidity funny. Sounds like a right good old time for sure. I find looking back that the drinking side of things was a real good time and I cannot lie to you about that. I loved the taste and the smell of it and a few creamy pints of Guinness were always second to none. Inside myself I just have a gene that is gluttonous or something because after the three or four sociable pints of stout I often found myself talking directly to myself in my mind while my mouth was to the pint glass gulping down the end of a pint, almost like I wanted the whole glass and everything inside of my stomach. I would say to myself "oh fuck I am getting drunk, I can feel it already. I better get some more" the more I had the more I wanted, like crack cocaine really if you think about it. The buzz was on and the only way to not let it get away was keep pouring more fuel on the fire. So could the argument be to look at a why or how?

Lack in self confidence - alcohol helps fake confidence

Feeling inadequate - alcohol helps bring fake purpose

Nervous & shy - alcohol removes inhibitions

Not comfortable in own skin - alcohol gives fake comfort

Self loathing - alcohol gives fake acceptance

See the pattern here, I am beginning to see a few but these were never a real big issue for me, none of the above anyway we'll not severely. There is something that is creeping into my mind and it is the escape buzz, feeling of a complete escape from reality that exists around you. The buzz to get away from somewhere and be in a different place and be a different you but surely this means there is something wrong with the you that you are? I should say the you that I am.

Seventeen and Life

Escape from life and the world and all the pressures from teachers and cops and adults all around just wanting and expecting me to be the perfect child with the best exam results and to obey the law in every direction and all the talk of how the bright future I have ahead of me and why would I want to throw it all away.

Now there is an idea, throw it all away. I have spent all my years being the best of everything, the best in sport and being the best in academics and where is the reward, I wanted reward and I wanted it now, so where was it? I could not see that the entire world was at my feet just waiting for me to blow up and grow up. The world awaits you is a very strong message to all of you right now who are reading this and are in the exact same position as me at sixteen or seventeen, or any age for that matter. The world awaits you is a true saying and statement for anyone, which says to me because this is the truth, it is upon me to make a stand or take a stand and go forward to become the absolute best I can ever be at whatever. It is upon me to make the changes needed in life to not drink and not bow down to a substance that can take from me and continue to take, not only from my emotional well-being but my health in general and my personality from me in the form of remove friends who might be very valuable and people that I do not need to lose in life. Alcohol can only continue to take from me and why do I need to escape from anything or anywhere. The perfect me exists right here right now. Who needs a reason to escape from reality so bad that upon landing yes the same reality exists yet now with a stack of problems even bigger than before and even more focus and attention from authorities and other adults who want to meddle in my life. Case workers, probation officers, group counsellors, psychologists and on and on the list goes. At twelve it was parents and teachers maybe even fun scout leaders and all of a sudden during a few years run it has changed and morphed into those above. Shit let me go back to school and start over, let me no longer look for the escape

Seventeen and Life

let me just be and be me. Yes I am the best I can ever be in any given day, what was I thinking? Chasing a buzz to escape and searching for a me that does not even exist, searching for a me to be better than I am and better than who? I am here now in jail, screwed up and hung over. The embarrassment now when I face in front of a judge again to plead my case and to answer the charges that are now before me. This time they won't just whisper rumours about me, oh no! This case now can go in the newspapers and be reported to the entire country for filling in print in their papers. I wanted to escape the happy life I have had from birth and the great family I was raised up in, to want to turn away from and beat my own path in life, become my own great man and wanted to do it all in a hurry. No adult was going to tell me what to do, no way, I was busy in a very fast track to self destruct and all under some illusion that this mighty alcohol made me some kind of super power and better version of myself. How dumb in fact does it all really sound?

I must remove alcohol, even though I cannot readily buy it tomorrow when they open my cell door, I must find a way to change this necessity to want to escape and be somewhere else. I just recognise the mighty Aidan that I am and that I have always been. Getting high and getting drunk what has that got to do with being the best me ever?

Of course nothing is the answer, oh yeah I know I just let it slip out about getting high and let it slip in the same sentence as getting drunk, so yes you are correct in noticing that and yes I did do a lot of drugs too, it wasn't just all alcohol. There, I just kind of opened the door to the topic of some very powerful drugs that brought about a whole and other part or new level to "how to escape" for even longer periods of time and sometimes without all the fighting and expense of sitting in the pub all day either.

DRUG OF CHOICE.

Is it something I am proud of to say I was a drug user? Not really but do I carry some shame in the area of life where drugs were an every day pastime? No not really either. A contradiction that even for me might be difficult to explain, ah sure we will give it a go.

I began smoking "joints" at as young an age as should be classed as highly illegal as I was around thirteen years of age. These joints were filled with tobacco and hash, what is hash? Hash is a product from cannabis and is other wise known as hashish. So these joints became a little more frequent and then pretty soon or more like before I knew it, I was smoking those "refer cigarettes" like any normal cigarette and I did not think anything of it. I can take a stand and a viewpoint that it had been a very fast spiralling downhill kind of route and hash was a must have just like having to have milk in your fridge, not something you think of every minute of each day but something that has to be there everyday and if you had none, it was a must to run out and grab some immediately.

The escape level was very similar to alcohol in a sense, a sense that some form of mind bending seemed to take place and when the brain became nice and cloudy then who ever had time for any problems?

In my teenage years thus far the drug names and list has grown quite significantly from just a few joints to a much wider variety of things. Not at all to glamorize drug use any or the getting high either from drug or alcohol use, I feel I would not be, being fair with you to not mention it at all and not discuss the elements of drugs use that seem or should I say seemed totally fine with me for a time in it all. The drug of choice as it can be referred to was hash and I felt like I needed to have it all of the time. I have listened to people being both pro and anti hash and I have thought about both sides of the argument and can only tell you that in my own personal experience that hash and the smoking of joints often seemed like a cool thing to do. There were times that having "the munchies" and satisfying the intense cravings were some of the closest feelings I thought I could ever get which resembles to me a visit to Willy Wonka's factory. It would also be fair to mention right now that I may be a touch of a chocoholic too. Being high and wanting to eat chocolate and crisps and drink minerals (soda) so when stoned I would go for a complete savagery session of chocolate, yes indeed a very pleasant time. Funny thing about being stoned is that nothing ever seems to register as being possible to enjoy as much when not stoned. Yet it is totally possible to enjoy and enjoy a little differently but more purely the same bar of chocolate, a stoned minds way of thinking just won't allow that possibility to exist, that it is possible to also enjoy and enjoy even more when sober, it has to be something about the demon nature in drug use and it's evil way of keeping your brain all muddled in between the high times. Another factor of the hash use was that if I had none I just felt like I needed to have some close at hand. Some hash to have in my pocket brought about a comfort level all of its own and this has nothing to do with using it or rolling any joints, it was just a new necessity and probably a mini drama or anxiety that I wanted to have. Having no hash meant being stir crazy until I could get some, I would not rest and found it impossible to concentrate on anything other than finding money to buy hash, when the hash was in my pocket somehow the universe seemed to be all in harmony and at peace with itself once again. That is pretty powerful in its own right just to either have it or not have it. I would have been a person who would have promoted the idea that hash should be smoked by everyone to bring about in a person's life a whole other type of understanding that I felt people just didn't know about because they did not smoke the stuff like I did. I wanted the whole world to know just like Jim Morrison or something, just get everybody to a state of high and then sure I won't have to even explain anything, people will just know. Again powerful stuff and it is considered to be innocent and harmless to have just a few puffs. Granted I was abusing the substance through my early teenage years already and probably was a little more than just a few puffs.

There were different kinds of highs attached to different kind of drugs and some were almost like outer body experiences and a whole lot more intense than my words could ever do justice to, just take my word for it, pretty intense is an understatement. Though with hash it is as if it depended on the type of hash you might have bought to what kind of stoned feeling you might get off it. Some of the feelings attached to being stoned were for example

Munchies "buzz"

Cleaning "buzz"

Giddy "buzz"

Lazy "buzz"

Vegetative "buzz" and so on and so forth, many different kinds of high could come from different types of hash from different parts of the world. It was this getting high that could make you do funny stuff like start cleaning and to do it so intense it made you like totally OCD about your cleaning. Nine times out of ten you never cared about cleaning anything but that one time when super stoned, the cleaning was on and it was intense, like you might even scrub a floor with a tooth brush. Makes ya do funny things alright. There were other types of being stoned with hash that would leave you in a condition or state that everything was funny or you just could not stop smiling. Keep on smiling at everything, walking down the town at home and just a big grin across your face and so much so that your cheeks began to get sore and hurt as they were almost like stuck and the grin / smile was not going away for the entire time of being stoned. My cheeks would really be sore and hurt from the "smile for the day" look.

All sounds good doesn't it until some of the more serious sides of the getting stoned as often as possible begin to show through and start to take grip over your life. The obvious one has to be that it is a gateway drug yet like the cliché says as it is from experiencing getting high and being stoned that the brain starts convincing you "what if you could get even more high, then that must be a better time" hence gateway because that will lead you on to other drugs and more serious issues, different highs with different side and after affects. The idea of being high seems so good to you that taking another drug and a different type of buzz can be experienced so now all of a sudden you are full on using drugs. Not just a few smokes here and there anymore but "full on" drug user. So the gateway side of the few joints does indeed exist, it is best said that if you do not want to end up using all kinds of drugs then it is probably best to not even try and think that a few joints could do no harm, they could for sure be that gateway to a whole other life that nobody ever planned for, drug use.

There are other nasty sides to this innocent cannabis product and it is like an automatic "angry" can occur when there is no hash. To go from waking up in the morning to see the day and begin life for another day with absolutely no reasons to be angry about anything and then after the first few minutes of being awake, not even giving yourself time to know what day or the week it even is, that first piece of your morning and then bang, you realize you do not have any hash. All of sudden you change to be a demonic type, angry can be an understatement in this situation. In that mode of being angry is just that anything can be a spark and turn on the aggression and anyone who might wish to engage with this other you will definitely get an earful or maybe even worse.

I had one of these more than once but will share one with you.

There were days when I woke up and went straight for my pockets to get a joint together and get a morning smoke in to me so that my mind could be high immediately and to be honest about it, getting high immediately after waking up just seemed to last for a long time and could stay stoned til well after lunchtime from that one little smoke first thing in the morning. This particular morning I remember going to my pockets and I knew I had a large lump of hash the night before but this morning it was not there. It was not the first morning that I had gone home the night before knowing I had some and woke up with none.

At first I thought maybe my brother had taken it and then started thinking about how bad it was if I was using this stuff on a daily basis and now my brother might be dabbling with it on account of me, the guilty feeling, though real was not enough or any way devastating for me to consider a change in my ways but I did feel a little guilty about this angle of thought just not enough as my main mission was to get my morning smoke. My brothers had all gone off to school and my parents had gone into the city to work for the day which left me all alone in the house and on the verge of going completely stir crazy over where is my hash. The best thing I could liken it too is when you know you are late for something and you cannot find your keys or even like when you know you have one hour to be somewhere and you cannot for the life of you find your bus pass. The time keeps ticking and the pressures of being late are on you and as it ticks by the search becomes much more intense and frantic, well that was me that morning looking under the beds on the floor, retracing my steps in and out the front door and the surrounding area of the outside and inside the doorway too. Behind the doors the bathroom and so on. The hash was nowhere to be found. I had spent like 40, last night to have some for the next couple of days and there I was without even enough for my little one skinner smoke for the morning, poor me, I know.

I searched everywhere and it was not anywhere to be found, the anger building up in me was not that I just didn't have any hash but I had spent my last money on it too and had no money to just go and get more. I knew I would be having a day of leisure and rest this particular day and had no plans to go anywhere so I used the last of my money just to make sure I had plenty of hash and would stay high all day, this was my plan for that day. I searched everywhere I could think of and my search had turned from half looking for my hash in the house to half looking for money too, if I had not got my hash then I need money to buy some more because my whole morning had crumbled apart and I was now full of aggression and super pissed off. The only answer that I could get into my head was that I lost it on the bus or walking down the road last night. I could not figure this out and even though it was not the first time that I had lost my hash I could usually tell myself it was because I was drunk the night before and could not remember why or where I was even. That day was different because I had a whole plan laid out in my mind, I was not drinking the night before and I was quite certain there was no way I could have just let it fall or drop anywhere.

There is a different aspect attached to using drugs too and it is that when you walk around carrying illegal substances on your person so to speak, you usually are fully aware of where they are and in which exact pocket and exactly how you are going to get rid of it at any split second should the police show up and decide they want to search you. So even though anyone on drugs can seem completely out of their minds and know nothing of what is going on around them, there is a very good chance they know exactly whereabouts their stash of dope is at all times. This would be why I was full sure I could not have just lost this piece of hash that day. I continued searching in places that I thought maybe my brother could have used as a stash spot. I stopped myself a few times in my search and would just sit and think and when I would sit and think is when the thoughts got more full of guilt, this is what they mean about how drugs can ruin a family? Now my brother is going to start using hash because he found it on me and the drugs are now in the family because of me and all life is doomed. Fuck that! I better keep searching was the only way I could get away from these mad thoughts. I wanted to rip up the carpet in the bedroom just to convince myself it had not fallen out and rolled and fell under the carpet where I couldn't see it or something. Thoughts in my mind to go out into the shed and get some of my father's tools and start ripping the house asunder. Where the fuck could my hash be? Looking back on this right now just reminded me that even though I thought I had it all together and my daily drug use of just simple hash was no big deal, I am remembering quite clearly that morning and how frantic I was to find the bloody stuff, it is like I was becoming obsessed or should I say a man possessed. I had traced my steps and it was not showing up.

Let me explain how big or what size a piece of hash for 40 pounds would have looked like, no not forty pounds in weight 40 pounds in money cause pounds is what we used in Ireland at that time. A piece of hash for that price would be approximately an inch and half long by an inch wide and maybe an inch thick as well, so it is not an entirely huge thing to be looking for. So in a house that might be, oh I don't know how large or small the family home is, let's say I am looking for something about 2 square inches in total size in a house that is about 1200 or 1500 or even 2000 square feet in size and with the possibility of having dropped it outside, well you can see the battle that was on my hands to get this search narrowed down

An hour I had spent searching and was getting madder and madder inside myself just because of all kinds of nonsense. Guilt for maybe one of my brothers could have found it, fear that my parents found it, anger cause I just wanted my smoke and be done and my day could be exactly how I had planned it but NO! It wasn't going to happen was it and now my day was turning out just shit and all angry. I am talking out loud to myself going around the house and it is the gritting of teeth so hard that they might break or biting down on your lip so hard it might even bruise, this is the beast that was now in full swing.

My search kept on though because if there is one thing drugs are going to do is give you ambition and drive about one thing really and that is, never give up a search for drugs. Using drugs will take away all other kinds of ambition but not the search for drugs and the wanting to get high. Don't let anyone tell me that drugs don't have a grip of a person so much that they can focus everything in their entire life about one thing and stay 100% focused. Drugs will make you screw everything up in your life from relationships with family and friends to do stupid things like breaking the law all for the search for the drugs. When you have them you begin thinking about how to get more and when you don't have them you stay thinking about how to get more and nothing else in life seems to matter. So even there I am showing you that it is a mess of a cycle of thoughts, once it was about having hash in your pocket and when it ran out it was time to get some more but then even having it was not enough to be satisfied and the madness of being fully consumed with thoughts around having to have it and when having some wanting more and needing more and feeling the need to have to be on the look out for money and ways and people to get more, somewhat of a never enough is enough problem all brought about by the hash itself and being stoned in the first place. Doesn't that in itself say or show how powerful it really is and why an innocent gateway drug just might not be so innocent at all?

So the hunting around the house continues and when in my parent's room I noticed that hanging on the closet door handle is a handbag of my mother's. Yes it is normal for a mother or a woman to have more than one handbag and so there would only be one she would carry to work with her everyday and others or extra ones would be in her room. The striking thing about this handbag was that it was the one she uses most frequently and my brain went cha ching! She must have forgotten her bag for the day and there might just be some money in it and my problems might be solved, just head on out and make my way to go and buy more hash. Not an immediate fix to my problems but a solution that the day had a chance to finish a hell of a lot better than when it started. I took the bag off the door handle and right away I knew something was up because it wasn't that heavy, as I laid it down on their bed to begin to go through it and just by its lighter weight I thought she must have bought a new bag and transferred everything because this has no feel to it at all. I opened the bag up and nothing a few receipts and paper work, no purse or anything representing money unless I wanted to try the cheque book, nah probably not a good idea. The inner of the handbag had like a silk type lining and a few zip pockets inside of it so I thought there might be some coins, maybe a few coins could amount to something of value. I was having no luck and felt like just throwing the handbag at the roof or somewhere, anywhere really. What on earth does my mother carry around in her bag anyway like nothing and although my hopes and dreams for a better day had been dashed inside of about sixty seconds, the anger was back on top and more like some lunatic rage now rather than just a soft simple anger. I pressed on and tore back a zipper of the lower pocket and there lay a foil wrapped piece of hash. I knew straight away it was hash and then another and another, these were ten pounds deals I recalled losing or misplacing some months earlier and then a much larger piece with no wrapping about an ounce of hash. I had been on a frantic search for a quarter of an ounce of hash all morning so far, driving myself crazy in the head and here in my mother's hand bag not a hundred feet away from me just only in a different room was a bag full of hash and hash deals, probably about a couple of hundred pounds worth of the stuff.

I had hit the hash lotto it felt like and to give an idea of my emotions, I sprung immediately into a plan of how my day had just gotten better beyond what I had thought it could ever be, from angry to giddy and greedy like an auld miser counting his pennies and laughing to himself, like I wanted to roll around in the stuff. Time to make a plan for the day the anger, where did it go? Where was all the madness that had my adrenaline running all morning go? Nowhere really I just was able to move directly into a mood of I have what I wanted and the getting stoned process was all back in play now.

It was mid morning now around about eleven o clock let's just say and I decided I will run a bath and have myself a nice "day joint" and just chill out, I mean after all that had gone in for me in the morning so far, I did deserve that at least to reward myself for such a stressful time. My thoughts also went to think of how daft my mother must have been to be walking around with a handbag full of hash and how she would have ever explained this if she had been caught up by the police ever, like they are going to believe she had been doing nightly raids on my pockets and explaining that to a police officer could get tricky considering there was quite a bit of quantity of hash and was also cut into little deals too, the amount would easily be enough to get charged with possession of cannabis and the deals would be enough to receive another charge of intent to sell as well. What on earth was she thinking?

I ran the bath and had another plan for after my smoke that I will make me a little lunch after I get good and stoned too. When I was sitting in the bath and smoking away I heard the front door of the house open and someone had come home. It was my older brother who had been on a half day from school for study purposes or something like that and he had let me know it was him by his shouting down the hallway at me about "what are you doing smoking" and his tone of disgust "what are you smoking". I had no plans for this and finished up my bath and my smoke, fuck him was the basic thought process there. A little more shouting exchange went on between us and I had gotten dressed, I was a nice and stoned too so having an argument with him was outside of my thought patterns as I wanted to enjoy my high, he kept on with his bickering though and so I went to walk into the sitting room where he was. We I pushed the door open it had gotten caught on the slight corner of the mat on the floor and it spring right back at me which caused the side of the door to strike me smack bang in the bone above my eye, it was like the funny bone kind of sensation just with a fuck load more pain. I turned immediately on the door and started kicking it and calling it a stupid bastard of a door and the more above my eye started to throb the harder I kicked it and swung my fists at the door eventually putting my foot right through the door. My older brother with his school books out on the floor and on his knees jumped to his feet quickly and shouting at me to "what are you doing and who do you think you are?" He was coming towards me too and we fell out of the sitting room in a tussle and into the hallway, I had the momentum and all the whole wrath of my morning was in full flight of being released which left my brother smack bang, dead centre of an outburst of built up angers that he wasn't ready for. We circled the hall and down to the corner of the hallway by the front door where I had him pressed into the corner and with a swing and some momentum from our scrap or fight the whole side of his body went crashing though the glass panel by the front door. Within only a few seconds I had put two holes in the door to the sitting room and my brother had gone through the glass of the front door panel. This was not the day I had planned at all. I had to call my father at his work and pretend the wind caused the door to slam and the panel beside it had smashed into many pieces. How I will explain the holes in the door, well that would have to be left until it got mentioned, the wind won't work for an excuse on that one. My brother was off tending to his shoulder as it had been cut by the glass and was bleeding quite a bit. Maybe this is what they mean about drugs causing havoc and destroying families. In a morning I had gone from happy to sad to mad and to completely happy and relaxed to raving lunatic full of violence and shouting to doing damage to the home and structural damage never mind any emotional traumas caused. I had stolen or intended to steal from my mother's handbag and wanted nothing more all morning than to just have that big smiley face that getting stoned was all about for me during those days but the "innocent gateway drug" had a ton of other emotional plans for me that day. From the harsh sickness of needing it to wanting it to craving it to having it to exploding with violent madness and then wreck the house. Here I am sitting and doing the hind sight on it all, well it does not appear such an innocent set of events at all. Makes me wonder real deep about the nature of what hash is or was and to what point have I fooled myself in to thinking that a joint here and there is harmless. HARMLESS my ass would be more like it. See what can become and what can be caused all by just a joint or two, not really the best idea at all. And I was one of those who would promote the use of such and think it was all okay. There are millions of stories to dig in to and go on and on about drugs use but as I am finding from one simple look back my best advice would probably be just stay away from the things and don't even bother to think to yourself, maybe I can get away with one here and there, not even worth the hassle not even close. The "say NO to drugs" campaign makes a lot of sense now. Does it make sense to you?

WHAT ARE EMOTIONS?

I often wondered and not just cause I am thinking back about drug use and what had happened that one day I couldn't get what I wanted when I wanted it but for more real reasons I wonder what are these things called emotions? What or how does it all happen and even more thought would be where do they come from, like do we have some kind of factory inside of us that produces "feelings" ?????

That deserves a lot more question marks than I have pages for but do you get what I mean? Sometimes I can be just sitting there and a feeling might pop up and totally out of nowhere a buzz or tingling comes over our bodies and spreads from our gut, sometimes even traveling down through our legs and up to our head. A feeling of what? So many or them all different and hard to even know what it could be called. Just like when we might read "a feeling came over me" we read that kind of sentence and somehow it makes perfect sense to us but at the same time it makes no sense at all. How weird is that?

To differentiate between our thoughts and our feelings can be difficult also and in some way we get confused between the two. I could ask you how do you feel now (Jesus don't say bored) but how are you feeling? Is it possible to think ourselves into a feeling or is it just the opposite that we feel our way into a thought? I have no professional letters after my name about this sort of stuff but I can tell you I have spent my years wondering about them and maybe even like you I have not given too much thought about them to be honest. Just kind of wondering but not actually getting into deep thought, kind of thing. After all it is feelings I am questioning and isn't it the right way to be on that subject, just kind of think a little about them and then close the door shut on them again. I can recall how I felt about many single events or incidents and remember well exactly how I felt during the time of whatever was occurring, I think back about this idea or concept of feelings to try and help tie some of the paths taken by myself to see if there is a feeling that has been a trigger or some significance to help me puzzle this piece all together. Yeah I know, piece of this puzzle together but because it is all about feelings puzzling the piece together seemed to be a little more fitting. Just like the "emotional well-being" of anybody, you or me or anybody. Who really knows what that is supposed to mean? What is healthy and what is sick or is there some form of healthy sick or a sick healthy, it makes a lot of sense if dissected but for those of us who just live and like to laugh when we can, well for us in a passing moment or a feeling moment, we don't have time to just dissect what the hell is going on.

I enjoy feeling most things and then when I feel pain or hurt I kind of hate it then a little bit and probably you do too. What I have learned in a short space of time walking around the planet is that a feeling no matter how hard or difficult it seems to be that it will pass away in its own time and usually as quick as it came on in the first place. I learned that it will not only pass on quickly but it has a relevant place in our life and shows up for its very own good reason and gives us a chance or an inkling of an idea that we are alive and living, a little reminder sometimes of how complicated we are, us human beings that is. Which does give me a moment to think about or spell it out a little bit.

If a feeling for us at any given time is complicated or we are not truly aware of where it came from or why then we would have to admit that we are for sure more technologically built than the computers of this modern day, we do not run on programs and algorithms nor do we have a predictive buttons built in and yes I know, many people are predictable in their movements or set in their ways but they certainly do not have any predictive text button. We are humans not machines and probably one of the few things that separates us from the machines and things around us in life is the simple fact that we have feelings, OMG! What a trigger word to get people going, mention feelings and some of your friends will almost climb out of their skin to over compensate that they do not really know their feelings at all, the other half of your friends might look for a subtle exit from your company and just slip away to the background (maybe more like run far and as fast as they can). It is a great topic of conversation to have and I highly recommend you have a good chat with yourself first about the how, the why and the where they come from before attempting it with your friends. Not to confuse our thoughts about our feelings with the actual feelings themselves. The lists of feelings possible is massive and hard to go into too many or each and every one but I have had some feelings that were quite strong from time to time that I just seem to have wanted to blur them out for a long time. I have met people who spend most of their time in the same circuit as me and in our time chatting about feelings they responded to me that they never feel anything and that they are like a rock or a stone or something and that all those feeling things are for women only and men have no place in the chat about feelings conversation at all either. Strange one isn't it?

Let's go back to the predictive thing though and see if I can make sense or that at all because really there might be a slight chance we do actually have something of that nature in us and it is so bizarre that I never noticed before. I have had many times where I had something important to do like make an appointment or be at an office of a probation officer for example or others were take up a new job, remember of course I had left school some years ago and the only way to keep a strong habit of getting high was to work too. Anyway why would I be late for something and why would I not just wake myself up and get busy with the day when I needed to be somewhere. What could be wrong that I did not care enough to wake up and be on time, I would have even turned off the alarm clock with a bit long sleepy arm making a grumble as I pressed the sleep or snooze button. Yes of course I might have felt like crap and didn't care as to the outcome of the meeting or whatever to the job, I will make an excuse and get another one. Some might have said I didn't care about anything and when it came to serious meetings I did not see the possible outcome or consequences of my not being there. So rather than face the day and the boring chores of conforming to what "they" all wanted I may have slept it out or over slept for that exact time. Yet on the same exact type of morning where I may have been drunk the night before but it was something that I really love to do like going for a little holiday weekend with the lads or a road trip which was going to be a lot of fun, then in those circumstances I did not even need an alarm clock, I awoke prior to the thing even going off, I would be awake almost just nearly waiting for the thing to start beeping so I could get going and begin my journey or my day. When I wanted to achieve something or get somewhere I never needed an alarm, I would wake within a minute or two of my alarm going off, why is that? How come when something with some importance to us, a holiday trip for example, if I needed to be at the airport for five a.m. I would have had my alarm clock set for three, somehow I would magically wake up at 2.58 a.m. without the need for the alarm at all. The predictive text button inside us managed to help me on times like the ones in my example. We have the ability to set our minds to a task or chore and tell ourselves that we need to be up by three a.m. and somehow the importance of needing to be awake and ready actually meant so much that my body and my mind would just wake up.

This definitely tells me that we or I have the ability to program myself into how things will work out for me in my life. I have the power within myself to tell myself how to be and when to be. I can remember being part of a group of friends and having different outings to go to and different fun weekends as a kid. When I was in the scouts we used to have different weekends away camping and these were very enjoyable times.

SCOUTS

When away for the weekend I remember clearly how at night when going to sleep we would be staying up late chatting amongst ourselves, they were nights where I felt very happy, the excitement of being in camp was great and the joy of being away from home and sleeping somewhere new all had a good feeling. The fact we were being well looked after by our scout leaders helped me feel safe and I guess really feeling safe as a child has a lot to do with being able to enjoy happy moments. We would have a camp fire at night with some sing along songs and everyone got involved. There was something about sitting around a camp fire and singing and even better were when our scout leaders would tell us some creepy stories too, nothing too bad to keep us up at night but very entertaining. As kids we had put our full trust in everything our leaders would say, I used to be totally engrossed in their words staring across the campfire at them as they spoke. The fire and it's flames made them look warmer in their faces and the dark and the shadows did not bring any fears or nerves or anything. These were real and genuine a feelings as any when I was a young guy and left loads of room for feeling safe and secure and happy.

Usually before we would head off for bed our scout leader would tell us the day that was planned for the next day and give us a run down of what time we were expected to be up and how far we are going to hike and whether it was in the forests or up the mountains and off to sleep we would go, always with a last word of warning "no messing and straight to sleep now guys, a big day ahead tomorrow". The hike our leaders had mentioned for me meant some fun times ahead and brought about good energy in me and excitement was added to just being on the camp and enjoying every minute of it. Such a simple time for a boy at nine years of age. When we were chatting as we were bedded down for the night & I remember clearly this one guy who kept on mentioning how he was not looking forward to tomorrow and he "hated hiking & especially up the mountains", most of the other lads were like me all excited and happy but this one fella almost as if to try and bring us all down or something he kept on moaning every chance he could get to speak. He did not want to go hiking and he was dreading the day, many of the other guys would tell him things kike,, "ya never know you might enjoy this one" or something like "if you try to enjoy it you will" and that was the key right there. Try to enjoy it, you just might.

We headed out for our hike and we had a great day in the woods and along the trails, yes okay there was mist and rain and plenty of dampness even along the forest floors. The little rivers and streams we crossed were also a bit of fun as some got a shoe or two wet through the day. Our friend, the guy who was not looking forward to it and was moaning all night, yes you probably guessed it, he did not enjoy himself at all. I figured you might think he gave it a shot and tried to like it but he just didn't. He moaned all the way up the mountain and all the way back down. He managed even to have some sort of fake injury by the end of it and was being kind of carried a bit by one of the leaders for the latter part of the hike too. The point to it all was I can recall clearly that day and how strange that he was having such a hard time and I thought how it made sense to me that he did not like hiking cause it was such a miserable time for him. For me it was the opposite, I loved every minute of it and we walked for miles and miles that day. My feet did not get sore like his nor did I even consider having to be carried on any part of the hike up and down the mountains.

We ran wild through the woods and even would tackle each other into the pine needles as they just seemed to be bottomless, pointy and prickly but it was a soft landing if you ended up head first in them. Nobody ever went too far ahead and only our negative nelly lagged behind maybe making the pace a little bit slower for the rest of us. He definitely was not trying to enjoy any part and he was just getting worse as the day went on, I even think our leaders were kind of getting sick of him too but they persevered. What young guy just like myself didn't enjoy this kind of a day? I did not understand fully what was wrong with him. I saw through other times growing up similar people that on some fun get togethers they were just negative and not looking forward to something and didn't want to be part of the soccer game on a Sunday or they did not want to go on the school tour with all of us kids laughing and enjoying our childhood. I did not understand fully or know, was it me that was wrong or was it right? It just made no sense, of course I was very young in those times but what did stick out were those guys who didn't look forward to stuff and moaned about it and that has been a valuable lesson to me through growing up. When they made it so that they just were not going to enjoy it anyway. The set themselves up to have a miserable time.

DECISION TIMES

We have the power to convince ourselves whether or not we are going to enjoy something or not. All the time we spend moaning about it and or complaining is a method for us to fully make sure we absolutely do not enjoy the event or day that is ahead. We have the power to bring ourselves down and we have the power to say "I am not looking forward to ...... And I don't think I will enjoy it", this is exactly what will happen because this is what we have told ourselves. So I now understand what was going on, we, people that is, have the ability to change exactly how we go through a day and how we enjoy it, if we tell ourselves we will not like it then the result is, we will not enjoy it. Sounds easy doesn't it? Just as simple as a few words to ourselves or even out loud and we have the power over our entire body and mind and feelings that we will not enjoy ourselves and the result will always be a bad day or a bad experience. Now this is some powerful stuff. We have the ability within ourselves to precondition our minds into a mind-set of how we are going to be, just like me setting my alarm clock and not even needing it because before I went to sleep I told myself, just wake up by the time I needed to be up. We can set ourselves up for failures by allowing ourselves to convince ourselves that we might fail. We can set ourselves up to have a horrible day just because we decided beforehand that is the way it is going to be. How mad is that? All it can take is a few words and we might not even know it is what we have done to ourselves, we can blame the rain or other people for how our day is, is all the fault of stuff outside of our own personal self but it turns out we have preconditioned ourselves to be miserable in the first place.

It sounds a hard sell or a tough pitch to say we have complete power over the outcomes In front of us and that we have power over how we feel about things but I have now grown to understand it and having witnessed it several times since my young days as a cub scout I have learned that we hold so much power over ourselves and our live's that it makes it hard to understand what it is when people say "I don't feel okay". Like why not ? What have you told yourself? I am not talking about being ill and having physical sickness although sometimes that can be avoided too, we sometimes can bring ourselves so far down with our negative and moaning thoughts that illness just landed right in the gap of negativity and can stay for a while. If I were to find myself nowadays saying I don't feel okay I am going to wonder to myself "what the fuck is that about", "what did you just say?" I am going to try and catch myself ahead of the spiralling out of control misery and correct my thoughts immediately on the spot. This is some of how we have the power to maintain and continue on a positive track, this is a method I use to not allow the "out there" circumstances change me or how I will not look for blame to other things outside of myself, be they people or events or just things. It is the power I have over myself, this is the way I can precondition myself. I have seen so many times in people how they can bring themselves down that it only stands to reason that I can bring myself up. I can take charge of myself and I can bring about a positive energy to my future by knowing inside of myself that it will be okay and I will enjoy it and I will be alright before during and after, well, almost anything really. I do not need to allow worry creep into my life and I do not need to allow fear take over my body and lead me down a path of ill health or sickness. Who would choose such a path? I guess there are just some humans that like to be miserable within themselves and it brings to them some kind of comfort or something, maybe they enjoyed a miserable feeling or they have a fond memory of how they were miserable and someone like their grandma always gave the warmest nicest hug when they were young and so they wish to have that warm hug again and the memory of being miserable first always led to that nice feeling afterwards so they seek it out and the end result is staying miserable in a hope to get that warm hug. ??????

For me I want to feel safe and I want to feel warm and loved and many of the nice feelings so I look for them and I go forward with some positivity in my attitude. Should I wish to be down in the dumps and all doom and gloom about anything then it will be doom and gloom I will have in my day. My choices and my decisions to feel how I want to be are hugely my responsibility.

Do you find yourself tired or run down or just feeling weird sometimes about what your day is like? Maybe try shirking off the negative feelings and maybe even try and get a positive light into your day that can help you feel just A O.K. it is possible and we have power over these things. A bit of a contradiction now that I hear myself say such a thing as I do not believe we have control over how we feel as feelings can just come out of nowhere upon us, yes I will still stick with that however we do have a power over whether or not these random feelings may be joyous and upbeat happy ones or whether they are down in the dumps and miserable ones. There is a difference. Determination is a great one for me and sometimes yes some times I have been too determined in the wrong direction maybe which has brought me to this lock up, this only helps me to know now like right now this very minute that BOOM!!!! my determination has been in the wrong direction, I need direction WOW! what a powerful word "direction" I have spent time determined not to allow the cops beat me at the game of Life. I have been determined to succeed in the wrong side of the law by selling drugs and using drugs by stealing on occasion and being in several fist fights. I have been determined to never let people get one over on me and so had to be always getting something over on them. I have been determined in the wrong direction.

What direction is there that I can set my sights on and what direction can I go to maintain a positive and bright outlook on my future?

MEMORIES TOO

Something I have often wondered is what is it about our feelings that brings us to feel one thing strongly and another a little less? I have loads of vivid memories and I wonder about what it is that makes them so clear as well as very "emotional" I guess would be the word or full of feeling. I think it is because and here is where all the wondering comes into play, I think it is that if I have a memory of the first time I really enjoyed a kiss with a girl, is it because I remember the first kiss and no others before that or was it the first time I had emotions involved in the kiss?

The first early memories of anything in our live's can be or are often the most vivid always, I would have to think yes but

Seventeen and Life

also how is that so? This would be a fair question for anyone to ask. I think back to many firsts and when I recall them I do get lost in the moment and have had times where the memory or reliving the memory can have as much feeling involved and around the memory that it is like it was just yesterday. My wondering is definitely about the connection I have had with memory and the feelings, is the memory real and clear or is it a weird version of the memory but because of the feeling involved the idea of the experience never changes? The feelings remain the same and maybe sometimes not as totally strong as the first time yet very similar in strength. So back to the kiss because that's why all the people kept reading this, waiting for naughty bits, this would be another piece where I wanted to enter laugh out loud or put an emoji in but decided against it really. I am sure you get the lol pieces anyway. Back to the kiss.

I remember kissing several times with my new girlfriend and I know I told you about some of those experiences earlier but here is the piece that brings about some ideas that may help me figure some of or all of this out. Me as any young boy would be thoroughly enjoyed kissing as a little fella and I thought that only the girls liked kissing as much but I can be honest and say I love it too. There is something about the way in which bringing noses closer together is like a sweet smell of the person you have young love for. Their scent perhaps or the softness of someone else's skin touching yours and of course not just anyone but the person you actually have "the hots" for. You move in closer and after brushing passed their nose with yours you then feel their lips, warm and soft again and moist but not wet, as all good love stories would tell you they are yes usually quite gentle and when you press your lips onto theirs there is a feeling of strongly pressed together but with a whole gentleness attached also. Another great contradiction in itself but is exactly how I remember it at least. There is that pushing together of the faces, lips pressed hard against each other in some form of lust or love or something that is just magical and electric. The warmth of their tongue sliding with your own tongue has some form of welcome to it like the invitation to bring more tongue and share the nibbling of each other. Our tongues tied together and playing games while almost forgetting to breathe is like a game I never wanted to end. When she puts her hands to the sides of your head and wants to bring you even closer in is like the whole world just stopped for a split second and you became the appointed almighty ruler of the universe. Is it passion or is it lust? I really cannot tell ya which but it is something that let all thoughts slow down for a moment and just enjoy. Yup simply enjoy the moment where your tongue is playing chasing games with your girlfriend's and she is holding you as close as you have ever been held before. My body seemed to know to control its own slobber and drool without having to think about it and how do our teeth know to stay out of the way naturally too? We both go the opposite side in the perfect movements and stay locked in this "embrace". A nibble on the tongue and a nibble from her too or a suckling of the tongue just with enough tension to heighten the whole thing even more. A feeling from within my whole body, warm and in love just like I have been served my favourite ice cream smothered in all my favourite sauces all at the same time. I smell her scent as I breathe softly through my nose and feel her nose brush against mine like I know she is enjoying the event also. Is the feeling so warm because I know she is enjoying this as much as I am and that is something that is new and I had never experienced before? To share a moment and a feeling together with someone and be locked together in the tongue chasing game that each one knows when to chase and when to retreat. I want to taste her and she wants to taste me, I want to dive all the way down her throat and disappear and have no reservations about how I look or how I may be performing. I am just sharing this time with my girlfriend and she is sharing it with me also. How beautiful can young love be? I can remember the moments and the kissing like it was yesterday and I can remember the best feelings ever seemed to roll through me like I thought I could fly or be something or somewhere else in a dreamland at those exact times.

So is the memory so nice and soft and warm feeling because it was my first time kissing with my girlfriend or is it a strong memory because it is the first time I had the feeling of being in love? This is the wondering part. If we have nice feelings attached to an experience that was for us a first time experience, is it the experience itself that helps us have the memory or was it the first time we ever felt that way and our memory has recorded the feeling for us and so the memory is so strong and clear because it triggers a feeling for us rather than the actual experience. Why even wonder about it I hear you ask and quite right too. I wonder about it because it would make sense to me that it is not just like a tape recorder or a video recorder or even our memory storing some sort of cookies on a data base in our mind just because we went through the experience like a computer or robot but it is recorded inside of our mind because of how we felt for the first time in that moment.

I think we can all remember our first times that we did some things through our life and we can remember clearly for example, I can clearly remember my first day at school, I cannot however tell you with the same certainty what my third or fourth day at school was like or how it felt but I can tell you in much detail about the first day. It seems to me that it is because that was the day that had a whirlwind of emotions attached to it and the feelings are what helped me record the memory in the first place. It is like anything really I can remember some birthdays and I cannot remember other ones, I think the ones I can remember are the one that had the deeper feelings attached to them and that then makes reason for holding the memory or our mind records it for us and we can be reminded easily as we will go through very similar feelings a billion times over in our life and the familiarity will be how we felt.

So is it the memory we remember or is it the feeling that we remember and then all the details fill in?

If it is just the feeling I had when kissing my girlfriend when I was a young boy then it would mean I would never have that feeling again only have similar ones but different every time I share a kiss with a girl and that would tell me that the first memory is the best but I have had some great kisses since then too, so why the memory does not hold as strong or were there just too many or them for them all to be remembered as special or magical?

If it is the memory in the mind that is the strong point then why would I feel when recalling the memory and why would I not have forgotten by now as the memory cannot surely keep all the data without deleting out some of the stuff as who could remember everything? Is this my opinion and many of you out there could be like in politics or something, half of the people see it one way and the other half see it the other? This is where my wondering comes from and leads me to believe in my opinion that it is the memory and the recollection of first time feelings that keep me feeling warm about these kisses. It is not my first kiss that I remember but more like the first time I kissed with feelings. And of course that would also mean that how can I remember yesterday if I had a "only so so" type of day with very little feelings attached. Some people might even say stuff like "I enjoyed it but I didn't have any or not much feelings attached..." So it is possible to remember something for what it was as it appeared in its physical aspect but when no feelings involved we just remember the physical side of something and how it looked or seemed to us at that time

I visited a church on several occasions as a boy and I remember many or them being meaningless and just a big old building where mass was being said and I remember they were cold and I wished for extra heating is how I can remember it. I can also remember visiting the very same church where I had feelings attached where I drifted off into daydream about how the artwork was hanging on the walls and wondering how the building was built and who built it and how amazing it all seemed. Imagining how it might have been in the images that hung from the walls and what is this for and what is heaven all about. Somehow the times I visited the church with the feelings attached seem to be more vivid and it seems that the more detached memory is the lessor of both types of memory. So the kiss was really magical and I can recall it so well because it is not just a memory I liked but it was a feeling I liked, the feelings definitely have a lot to do with a whole bunch of how we see things and where we go with our decisions based upon how we remember what feelings we felt.

Animals are easily trained, well usually anyway, but they are easy enough trained and their training quite often revolves around food. We take a new puppy out for a walk and they begin to have maybe their own memories of the beach or the park and we can see how happy they get when they get back to their favourite places. We trained them to come back to us with little treats and so do they have a feeling memory of the walk in the park or they just know they are going to get treats now?

We humans on the other hand will keep coming back for a feeling over treats and when we feel something nice we probably will want it to reoccur as often as possible please. I recall my first kiss with feelings for sure, not just my first kiss or my fourth kiss or fifty third either but the first one and to be fair I would have to say my first ONES that had feelings. They were absolutely wonderful.

I almost got lost in my own memory there and forgot to keep typing.

Seventeen and Life

Yes the kisses were wonderful and the feelings just amazing but to tie it together with some of what I seem to be getting closer too all the time in my look back and how to piece it all together to try and make sense of what the fuck am I doing in prison does not have much to do with the beautiful memory of the kissing, it has more to do with me beginning to identify that the feelings are what have been my game of chasing so to speak. If it is that I have the very best memory of getting high then of course it makes perfect sense that I chased the feeling. I wanted the feeling I had the very first time to be relived over and over and over. When I got drunk I was so completely transformed to a new me that I wanted to be that new me all of the time and enjoy those feelings that my memory had recorded for me. Not just the feeling of being shit faced wasted but the multiple feelings as they become distorted through drinking, the levels of changes when drinking is like begin all excited and enthusiastic and then transform to a bit giddy and happy to then a little hot in the head and then on to confused and the laugh at anything stage, then ending up disorientated and puking and wobbling and all kinds of messed up. I don't think any of us wish to drink ourselves to that wobbly or more like staggering stage and no one wants to drink to puke but I would hazard a guess that we do want that buzz through a few of the earlier stages for sure.

I really am beginning to piece some stuff together here for sure and I can definitely say that I want the feelings revisited. I know what feelings I want and I have always wanted to just relive them and keep on enjoying life. Keep on smiling and keep on laughing. How can it be that I had to be as I mentioned so determined maybe in the wrong direction and have chased the high so far down the rabbits hole that now I have found myself locked up and in total darkness. Not darkness of without those poxy fluorescent lights but the darkness inside of my own person. The darkness that is the loneliness of looking around a prison cell and wondering all about these things in the first place. What I do know is, I do not have any proud feeling attached to where I am and if this is the first time of this feeling I sure hope that this is not one that I want to relive or do we have a mechanism that can automatically recognise a shitty feeling and makes us steer clear of it for all of the future. I would have to think that there is a preconditioning possible to train itself in a way that prison becomes a no for the future. Let's make it a real NO.

Maybe some of those guys in the other cells got the happiest feeling they ever had when they got to prison for their first time, like a "I've made it" kind of feeling for them and now they just spend their life going in and out of prison because they too are chasing that first memory of their first time having that wonderful feeling for themselves.

Who knows, right?

MAKE a CHOICE, TAKE a STAND

A great intro into a speech or a classic quote used to be "there comes a time in every young man's life...." Well I suppose it comes to us all at some stage be us young man or young woman that we must make choices and decisions and not just those ones about "oh will I go the shop or will I stay at home" or any little ones where we do not have a big deal involved so they are barely even decisions, yes they are decisions but I am talking about the big decisions about what we want to do with our lives or what we are going to choose to do for the long term of our life. Those decisions we make and we fully intend to stick by them. The committed decisions that we make. Some people get married, we see those people everywhere and I am quite certain they probably didn't just jump into that scene on a whim neither. They made a decision to do something and it was a decision to stick with for a long time (yes on the more than average basis as I know some do get divorced pretty soon after). But making decisions is a piece of our life that we may not change too easily or not just to go back on our decision too quickly and so we probably need to take a bit of time to make them in the first place.

I can clearly see that my own decisions have been of the not so bright side as they do say, "take a look around you if you wanna see where you are at in life" well I just did that and it is showing me, Yes! My decision may have been a bit flawed in my choosing of which dreams to follow and which decisions to stick by. But hey, life is a long old merry-go-round so maybe there is still a chance to alter the course of this life stuff and make a few decisions that could lead to better places.

I already have some prison tough man stuff up my sleeve for in the morning like, hit the biggest fella and take him down (that will earn me respect) or just to bananas and tackle down one or the guards (that will make me a talking point for the other inmates and get me some peace) I also have thought about just trying to keep my head down and say nothing to nobody, make no eye contact at all with anybody. Keep my mouth shut and do not fall for any teasing or taunting. Perhaps I can take a different approach and the minute I walk out that door in the morning is the beginning of the new me.

I have the power over how I interact in this situation and it is with my decisions that I can either make it all work and go from this bottom to a new high. A decision needs to be made and one of those life decisions where I make it and I stick by it all the way. Do I go deep into this prison life and stake a

Seventeen and Life

claim in the criminal world, a kind of let them know I have arrived and I am here to stay so don't fuck with me because I am not afraid to stay here for the rest of my life or stay real quite and not get involved, stick to myself and walk out that door with my head down and only respond to any attempts to rile me up with my head down and a slow motion to my walk. Take it all in as I walk and be nobody's fool but keep my observing eye working overtime for me to see where I might catch my breaks. Yes a decision is needed and there is nobody here in this cell for advice either. Just me and my mixed up head and a whole bunch of life searching memories. How can I draw on all this to make it in this world I now find myself in? Oh it is the same world that you are living in, yes that is for certain, only mine has been a little turned upside down right now and is nobody's fault or anything other than my own, so what's it gonna be?

Seventeen and Life

We all make decisions in life and some are so petty it can be just a simple spur of the moment thing and what we decide has very few consequences to how it might affect our day or our life in general and then on the other hand we choose every little step every minute of everyday whether we realize it or not. Each little thing we do has some sort of knock on effect to where if we turn left or we turn right means we meet a different person on that street than the other or we see a different clothes shop and we go in and buy something different and then that leads us to looking great on a night out where we meet the person we were meant to meet had we turned left that day but this time we are better dressed and so the person we meet treats us differently and becomes a wife or becomes a boss in a job or whatever. We could have turned left that day and met that very same person under a whole other bunch of circumstances and then they would not have become our wife or our boss. This would suggest that the decision we made on that one day to turn right was the right decision as it led to a better outcome, though the outcome was not directly In front of us that given day. It did all roll and weave its way together for the better of us in the long run though. Does it mean that had we turned left we might not have met those people, probably not or does it mean we would have not bought that particular outfit and looked different at a party and met the same people in the same way or would have met other people and boosted us even further in our life? Hard to know isn't it?

Our little decisions have the domino effect maybe even much more deep than we could ever understand as after all we are just human. When faced with a cross roads in life, is it the b all end all of how it will become further down the road or is it just and intersection like any other and what we choose, left or right means nothing to us or our future? Here I am faced with some real decisions to be made and I feel that they will shape the exact nature of my future and yeah it is the first time I probably have even considered the whole thing as a type of map it all out kind of scenario for my life. Here I sit at the crossroads of 17 & Life, am I at a crossroads of life or just another intersection?

How can I know what the future holds and how can any of you know? We can't I suppose would be the best way to put it as we are not fortune tellers and we do not have insight and depth to figure that far in advance. I have read in different articles in the newspapers and stuff or seen people on TV that have been quoted as saying they knew exactly what they wanted to be and they stopped at nothing until they got to complete their goal or their dream life. Seems a bit far fetched in terms of real life but they are out there and supposedly exist. I cannot say I have some life goals in mind right now and I do not have a clear vision of where I ought to be, maybe you do have one and that is absolutely great. I hope to be there some day, for now it is about weighing up the options the best way I can see them. Maybe you too can take a look at your surroundings and what options you have at making something different happen and bring about real change. Changing something does not have to be drastic or over the top in any way just a little tweak here and there could be the perfect remedy to bring about some extra luxury of contentment in a difficult world.

So what can you or me do to understand what making a decision might be all about, I would have to figure that it is all about weighing up a few options and seeing which one might work out best for us, maybe even trying to have a little insight to the future although that might not be totally possible, it can be looked at again with the robot aspect, we are humans and not anything like a robot and I don't think anyone really has their life mapped out and calculated so precisely that they stay in constant rigid stress to make it all happen exactly, that even sounds like a whole lot of no fun at all. Would it be worth the stress to make a plan and devout ourselves to a life decision so much that we make ourselves sick or ill in the process of being determined not to allow ourselves a little wriggle room to falter from a plan or decision we make. Of course we can and we can make a decision and change it later if we are not getting the desired results. That is the beauty of our power and ability to choose, we can change our minds anytime we feel like it too. There is though the times like I have myself in that some decision has to be made one way or the other, it cannot be avoided. I must find a path or find that right street to walk down and can only live in the hope that I choose well. If I do not choose correctly here is to hoping I can make a new review about all a little quicker than I have done to date and readjust accordingly.

So weighing up the options. Continue on a path of self destruction and a path which obviously does not feel like the smartest move I have ever made in life because looking back through times past, right? kind of highlights some way far out there messes are in my wake and not the best life for a young man to have lived. That really does sum up the so far piece of the so good expression. Time for something new. It does not seem so strange today about making a new start and correcting my ways, maybe you do not have to get to where I am to reflect and make alterations to your own life. Maybe it does not take a prison cell for everyone to start realizing that life is on the wrong tracks.

I guess making a decision is really about telling ourselves or more like convincing ourselves that we have been defeated on the path we have chosen and it is not something we can keep up with, we cannot keep banging our head against a wall and hope that it will just crumble and that we will be without injury to enjoy whatever it is we believe is on the other side.

Am I kicking myself for my life choices so far and what decisions have led me to where I am at right now? No, I am proud of myself to have began to reflect and look back and see that the path I had chosen has been full of wrongs or more like the wrongs have outweighed the rights, this is what it has taken to lead me to where I am and that is not as much about the cold prison cell as much as it is about the remorse and the guilt inside of me. The soul searching time I have to reflect and consider a new path for the life ahead. Back to the feelings again, the feelings have been aligned with my mind and some moments of clarity have come to me, what better way to make a life decision than in a time of clear thought. What the future holds who knows but what I can be certain about is I must change the method I have been operating with and find a new way forward. I am going to have to commit to this and stand by my decision if this new road is the road I want and I will have no room to be mad at myself for the decision either. I can already feel by writing this out to you that you are willing me forward on my journey and for a better one too. I just hope you too can see that there are many twists and turns for all of us out there and that maybe you can make a decision of change for yourself too along with me.

17 & Life.

Seventeen and Life

We have the power and ability to precondition ourselves so we can be certain in ourselves that we will succeed in any new decisions and we will not have a hard time standing by them either.

How we feel about any new hurdles along the way can easily be overcome or enjoyed rather by letting the feelings in and sit with us for a while and getting to know them and what it is like to think clearly with our minds of how to deal with any ups and downs that occur. I have the power to take charge of my destiny and how I deal with all that lies before me, it will be fine no matter what and I will see the benefits in everything I do.

I am beginning to feel better already, some fog may just be beginning to lift and who would have ever thought that by sharing my thoughts with you that I could begin to see more clearly how strong I am actually am, I hope so much you are beginning to feel it too. How simple a process can be when we have that moment to bring it all together, the how and the why of our own actions and some thoughts towards how we do actually feel about ourselves and our life. What does it all mean to us in any one given moment and what are the things that we repeatedly allow to keep us down? What are the things that hold us back and what are the negatives that we repeat to ourselves through little whispers in our mind that continue to keep us from making that decision, those thoughts within ourselves that bring about some doubt that we cannot achieve or we cannot reach our goals. It is pretty simple really, make goals for ourselves that we CAN reach. Make decisions for ourselves that we have no hard time sticking by, make choices that we are willing to uphold and know in our heart of hearts that we have taken a true honest look at ourselves and our situation, we know that we do not intend to hurt anybody and we know that we are forming our decision based upon a deeper look at our future self and where or how we see ourselves in that very same future.

I have never seen myself in many situations that I have ended up in but now I can say with true clarity it is because I never really looked. Wow! You know this last while I never even noticed whether there was noise outside or not, as I listen around it seems like everybody must be finally asleep. It is much quieter now that I am paying attention, I thought it was just my new breakthrough about how I must proceed and what I should do and how my outlook has gone from bleak to very bright, very bright indeed. There sometimes has to be a low spot and a low point in order for us to seek out something clear or a clearing of the clouds to allow us to just view it all and take that position of power back over our life.

Making a decision to change seemed like a complete and utter nightmare before and now it is like the most natural thing I should be doing. How amazing is that? No seriously, try it. Wow, AMAZING!

GOOD PEOPLE.

Is it possible that everyone and anyone is exactly that, just anyone or is everybody somebody? I like to think that everybody is somebody and no-one is a nobody. Isn't it fair to say that everybody deserves recognition for their good stuff and their strengths and if at all possible to lend a hand when you see someone struggle with maybe what is or could be considered a weakness. Do humans have the ability to change?

I have been quite bad in my times of abusing myself and my body and sometimes even other people's bodies (fighting) but it is fair to say I was not born bad or I never meant any harm to anyone when I was growing up. I believed in hard work and earn for the hard work so that I could enjoy the fruits or my labour. Hard work seemed like the honest way to be when I was growing up and seeing the older men and women going to work and coming home late at night. There did not seem to be any particular reason that stood out in my mind as to why they did such long hours working except to enjoy their time off I guess. I never saw someone else's struggle or had any idea how difficult it might have been for some.

Seventeen and Life

My own dad was and it goes without saying but I will say it anyway "one of the all time greats" there are those who are going to push you to your potential and you will probably not even notice them doing it until after they have long gone.

There are those who will for no other reason than they enjoy a smile and will love to share in any of your good news and your achievements. There are those that will pat you on your back when you complete your tasks and you didn't even know they noticed the struggle you had been through, who knew they were aware. There are those who work in the background and out of your sight just to see you alright and they wish for no recognition at all. There are those who at all times will defend you to anyone who wishes to speak ill of you and will never be known to you, of course because the person that would speak ill of you will not coming running to tell you how that other person stuck up for you and spoke in your defence. There are those who will just smile and bid you hello with a smile and respectfully not concern themselves in your business but are so delighted to hear how you are doing so well. There are those who will think of you and pray for you and though you have not engaged with them and have not even spoke with them for some time, they will always have you in their thoughts.

The tricky part of all this is how on earth do we know or recognise who exactly they are? Good people come at us in the most unusual ways in our life and sometimes those we think are just no good at all can end up being the exact opposite, quite hard for your too know or recognise them when they are genuinely doing their own job or casually involved in your life as if they have nothing really to do with it but they are routing for you every step of the way. Sometimes a friend likes to hear your stories or smiles when you smile and this can work wonders for your own journey, how do you know who is real and who is fake?

I have to think back on the times I was in trouble and had the police breathing down my neck, as you already know I did take on quite a few fake charges from the system and had a tough time with them because there were many charges that were real and genuine too. So when I was arrested and giving my testimony that I was innocent and had nothing to do with any or the charges they were trying to present to me all the while my "friends" were right next door spilling the beans and giving up all the information to the police. Now if that is not about as comical as one can make a true story, then I do not know what is. I hold no resentment and I put it down to the innocence of my friend at the time but man o man what a way to make that mistake about who is real and is one hundred percent and who is not. I know I was complaining earlier on about the police and some of the situations I have had with them in the past and I still believe they, the actually police who beat me up, are nothing but scumbags to this present day, they were supposed to be the good guys and the ones to look to for help in a crisis or to be the stand up guys in the community and I just want to make clear I am not saying all police are but definitely the ones who thought it fun to beat up a teenager for fun and then screw their life up with fake charges, well there ya go that was not hard in those times to figure out who was the real scumbags, scumbag is just a very Irish word for dirt bag.

So I had learned I could not count on my friends to keep their mouths shut in the police station at the time they were supposed to be stand up guys and I also learned that those cops of the time were filth. I mean cops who were supposed to be trained and on their way to careers and be responsible adults all dressed in uniform for work every day and they were worse than the dirt bags of the streets, so it was not hard to spot the good guys from the bad guys through those two examples alone. I guess the point being if ya pay attention to what is going on around you it is easier to spot the loyal and trustworthy ones from the fake and the good guys from the bad. Again just in case any of my friends who might have "ratted" on me back in the day it is only fair I make the statement again, I HOLD NO RESENTMENT, I hope that public shout out can set the record straight and sure while I am at it, it is only fair I make another public statement to those who beat me up while wearing their police uniform YOU ARE AND WLWAYS WILL BE ONLY SCUM.

Feels good to get that of my chest.

The good guys though, at least I can say even my friends and me at the time were little trouble makers on a small scale, well at least they have grown up a bit now and are doing alright for themselves, that is a good thing. I wonder could the same be said for the cops?

I had received a probation term from the courts right at around those times of fifteen and some of the terms involved was that I provide urine samples weekly to see was I using drugs anymore or not and weekly visits to counselling. I made sure not to miss any appointments but I cannot honestly say that some of my urine samples may have been a bit dirty and on one occasion I showed up to the counsellor's office all high and stoned. He let me sit for a minute or two and then he looked at me with a smile " you might as well go" I thought that was nice and easy for me, a simple session but he followed up with a few words more "don't ever come to my office high again and if you wanna stay high maybe we should see if the courts want to just take you out from my program altogether". My thoughts on him that day, remember now I was a fifteen year old punk who thought no one even knew when I was high. I thought I kept it well hid, to the trained and experienced eye like his, well it was as obvious as an elephant on a pool table. I thought, what a fucking prick for wasting my time and the real truth or the situation is I was just there wasting his. Even though I was by order of the court to attend his office I felt and quite truly thought it didn't say I had to attend clean and sober so what is his big problem? He had a look of disgust on his face too as he spoke to me across his desk in his little office. I thought fuck you man I am out of here and I won't be wasting any more of your time that's for sure. I didn't get it that I was big time wasting his time and he had been appointed to me to work on me not using drugs so I guess I couldn't have insulted him much more than I did by showing up stoned.

That man's name is Jimmy judge and if anyone out there ever knew him or knows him, well let me just say he has to be a single Saint sent from heaven because even though I screwed him around and insulted him by my actions he did not let me down when I needed it and he spoke so highly for me in court I could not even believe my own ears.

That situation with him that day in his office did not ruin my chances with him and even though he was disgusted at me that day he saw his work to be more important than my young punk attitude. There lies my friends an example of one of the good people in life. I hope he doesn't get too upset that I mentioned him either or the Ballymun youth action program, I think that is what is what called.

The other thing to note or what I learned was not to think people were fools and going around high and stoned was obvious to probably a lot more people than just my youth worker at the time.

Ya just never know the good ones out there who work day in and day out trying to save a youth like myself from themselves and the path of self destruction that we obviously had no idea we were on. This could probably apply to adults too, it does not have to be just youth but I am speaking from a youths point of view of course. The good people are on every corner and in every day that we live, we cannot spot them and they do not wear any bright clothing so it might not be a bad idea to just believe in humanity and that there are good people everywhere. Probably would do no harm to keep a policy on board that says, treat em all like good people until they show you otherwise. Why not? Might be the best chance at surrounding yourself with not only good but great people in your life. I think it is a good idea and something I am going to keep with me as I proceed further along this road of changing my ways and changing everything that has brought me to prison in the first place. Good people who have shown support deserve it for me to start making an effort, shit, I deserve it.

QUIET MORNING

The only noise around me for the last while has been the prison guard's shoes clicking and clocking along the landing. He must do a timed route to check on everyone's cell or something. I was so distracted by my thoughts I just have missed him peeking in a few times or something but I hear his shoes approaching now again. Imagine if he knew what was going on inside my cell and what it is that I am thinking, do you think he would just open the door and let me out? Nah probably not. My only path out of here now will be through court cases and a whole heap of bullshit, probably have to prove myself and my worthiness to be allowed back in society, sucks for me...

The other sound that has come into the air are birds, birds are chirping and sea gulls can be heard off in the distance squawking away, so they are awake which means morning is in full swing. Every prisoner seems to be still sleeping, I have no idea what the drill is going to be once they open that door. Do I get jumped by them other inmates or do I report for some kind of duty or something? I have no clue, what do inmates have to do during the day anyway and how do I go about finding who I need to speak to about making appeals to the courts to get out of here. Oh Jesus I have completely forgot to think about making a plan of action to get me out of here as quickly as I got into the place.

There are still sounds of delivery trucks out on the streets but there are a few more now and I can hear more city busses too. The world is waking up out there and loads of people will soon be off to work for their day, traveling up and down the street right outside the prison gates. Do they stop and think of the inmates and how much is going on for my life right now? Do the commuters know that everyone in here is wishing to be where they are right now, free and on their way to work on a cold quiet morning in Ireland, they have no clue the jealousy inmates have of them and their freedom and I

Seventeen and Life

guess those morning commuters if asked would probably reply that it was each and every one of our own decisions that led us here so they cannot have compassion towards us. That's what I am now, an inmate of the prison that lies somewhere inside a few stone walls which are the perimeter that runs along the street front.

For you a quiet morning in this part of town might mean a cup of coffee whilst waiting for your buses or a walk along the street to the next connecting bus to head off in to work. We can hear your footsteps almost or maybe it is just the way in here plays with your mind and we just imagine your shoes on the pavement. The cars coming to a stop at the traffic lights and the ticking over of the engines. The deeper hum from the trucks and the distinct noise of the city buses, yes that freedom out there has a lot of unique sounds alright. More signs to tell me to question a little deeper the why I fucked it all off in the first place, my own freedom that is. I am not asking that everybody who beats their way along the pavement outside should spare a thought for the inmates but I did want to share with you how all of sudden when inside this little cell of how the mind starts to imagine you walking by, imagining you have bubble gum and cigarettes and comfortable clothes and probably took a nice long hot shower this morning too. You didn't spend your night starring at little mousey or drudging through your every mistake in life. In here you imagine so hard that freedom out there, that the thought of it almost brings smells to your nose that aren't even there. How mad is that you might think, if you were where I am inside a little prison cell you would see how absolutely not mad at all that it is, how conceivable it really is.

There is no real format to share with you exactly what it is like, right now is quiet and I can only imagine the mad house it is going to turn in to shortly. This is what I have to prepare for at seventeen years of age, I have no worry about being tough or how many or them there are outside the door when it opens. As far as I am concerned I am the toughest person on this landing and if tempted I hope not to have to prove it. I want to maintain this positive thought process and begin working hard to getting out of here. So I for right now am beginning to enjoy already the image I have of freedom again and what it might hold in store for me. Some of the thought processes required to keep myself from never having to return to this place.

Maybe the next quiet morning I ever enjoy will be with the same kinds of clear thoughts only next time clear thoughts and just sit to watch people go hurrying on their way to work or maybe even on my own way to work, out there. I have only spent five or so years working hard on getting myself into this place but it has only taken five minutes to know full sure the only place I want to be is out there and enjoying that quiet morning with all the rest of society, Free.

POSITIVE UPSWING

Seventeen and Life

I wrote this out for you to read and of course the fact we have made it this far makes me oh so proud to know you are reading about my deeper thoughts and times in life when it all seemed in turmoil. I of course hope that something tiny will maybe touch you and help you to get some thoughts straight in your own mind as I have spent doing my whole night long. I was a very bitter young man walking into this prison last night and none to happy of course but my bitterness was towards the authorities and all who had no problems placing handcuffs after handcuffs on me. From the police handcuffs on me as I left the police station to the new cuffs of the holding cell below the courthouse and then to the prison officers handcuffs to enter the prison van. The judge as he mumbled to the police in the court, a special sitting of the court just for me, no other hustle and bustle in the courtroom just me and anyone else in there for the whole evening were just a shower of bastards as far I was concerned, all of them getting in the way of me and my freedom. I did not see that I had brought about this vacation away and locked up out of society. I just saw that I wanted to keep on going with how I see fit and they, the whole lot of them see things a much different way.

I guess my real anger was at myself and being hard on myself for letting myself down, I did not ever want to go to prison and yet I did not do enough to stay away from the place. For me it is this prison cell that has brought about my reason to even share with you but I guess it is only a physical place and the real prison is inside of ourselves. Our minds and our feelings, these are the only things that can truly imprison us. If you feel like life has not been treating you fair and the whole system is out to get you as an example, I guess I want to take this opportunity to share or express to you my new found ambition and new goal for a long life journey. Take a little moment for yourself from time to time to breathe,

Seventeen and Life

breathe in life into your lungs and your heart, let that free oxygen fill your lungs and allow them the chance to do exactly what they are designed to do. Breathe in that air and taste it, feel it as it fills your nose and down into your chest, know that as it does so it is bringing new life to all of your cells in your body. Allow your heart to receive the new oxygen and pump it all around your body. This is what the body does. Sometimes we forget to think for a minute and sometimes we forget to breathe. Breathe out your troubles as you exhale, allow all that waste and negative energy to leave your body. Breathe out the hatred and the bitterness, allow your mind to get clear. Try it a few times, like three or four times to take a long deep breathe and just focus your mind's eye on that breathing. With every breath in comes new life, new air and new hope for your future and as you exhale feel the bitter taste of all your hatred and confusions travel out from your body, out from your mind.

Try it, try and find a quite space to sit quietly by yourself, you do not have to be on the verge of going to prison just to need to take a little time to bring your emotions and your mind in line. It is only what I have learned by my experience that can help you with yours. To repeat the prison we all have within us is a feeling of greater torment than where I am physically at the moment, my prison is of bricks and mortar that is. But there are so many who carry on each day out there with all the freedoms of society and living within it but yet are very much in prison themselves. If you find yourself at war with your thoughts and an emotional pot boiling over then do for a moment try and do this breathing exercise, it will help and this I can promise.

Take in the good air and allow your mind to slow down. With each new breath comes new air, new life and new hope. This is important to remember.

To take the time to slowly focus on how your body enjoys this new air is a massively important step and you may find you are beginning to become emotional for what seems no reason at all. Allow the emotion to travel up with your exhale and allow it to leave your body with the air you are breathing out. Let all that nastiness and bitterness out every time you breathe out. This is an exercise that can bring you maybe even to cry and that is totally okay cause just like me maybe you are at a crossroads in life and maybe just maybe there is a piece of you that needs it to help you gain a clear sight of what needs to be done as you move forward to your next phase. My breathing exercise has been to write this all out for you, and even though I have said for you well it really has been for me. This has been my time to reflect and recall what and where I may have slid off the rails so to speak. My moments to reflect on what is it that may have brought me to this crossroads in life and such a major one for me at only seventeen. It doesn't matter at what stage or level you are at in your years, if you can find some small time to try and slow everything down to some simple breathing and allow your body to just be. Stopping your mind from racing and bringing about some emotions will be the healthiest thing you can do for yourself, to get some clarity both from how you feel and for between your ears. Sometimes our struggles go unnoticed and nobody knows any pains or thoughts that we carry inside of us. The pain of prison is horrible and if you are suffering inside of your own prison, please do try and do the breathing, it may just help you to reach out to somebody and share your words with someone who can help you by just being there. There are those good ones that do exist.

If you are having a tough time and are confused about where you are heading try and read back at what I was sharing with you,

We have the power to precondition ourselves to begin to feel good about where we are heading

Feelings come and they go and cannot consume us beyond what we allow them to.

There are good people out there, trust your gut. It is not failure of your choosing of a friend who let's you down.

Breathe and breathe well and allow this prison, just like mine, let it be the catalyst that maybe we needed to launch to a new level of understanding ourselves and realizing we do deserve our second chance and have confidence in knowing that by deciding to press forward and take on the changes, people will recognise it and your efforts.

You are appreciated.

THE DOOR OPENS.

I would be some piece of shit if I told you now that, that was all just a dream I had last night, maybe time to change the pillow and the mattress if those were the kind of dreams I was having. It is not a dream unfortunately for me and prison is very real. If you find yourself moving closer to prison each day of your life, please do take my word for it and begin your changes and your decision making before you have to end up here.

This is not a dream and is all very real. I can hear the prison guards walking the landing shouting orders now and there is banging of doors and keys jangling. He is going to open my door soon, by the sounds of things he is on the floor below mine. It is already sounding like a canteen or a public swimming pool on the busiest day of summer, the humming of voices is too much to make out any one conversation. Soon it will be my door that opens, what do I do? Stand ready to rush out or close my eyes and pretend to be asleep? My new life of prison is upon me and I am ready (I think). This is all very real and is happening and I am about to be unlocked for my first day, this is not junior school and me crying will not get me a minder today. Oh shit!!!

My whole night left wondering and sharing with you, I thank you sincerely for sharing the time with me and helping me to figure some stuff out, I hope you can figure out some stuff too by our sharing this time together. I have a very clear mind of what is required and what I need to change to turn this ship back around and begin again. I am only seventeen and I do have my whole life ahead of me. From now it is right choice of words and stay true to myself. Give myself the breaks I deserve and take everything in my stride. I really mean it, your support is totally appreciated and I am glad to have been able to share with you. I searched my mind for where or how it all went wrong and I found not much to indicate a pinpoint trigger. Sometimes life just happens that way and where we end up did not mean it is where we stay or where we must remain. We have the power inside of us all.

Here are the keys outside my door, "step back over by the corner of the bed" he shouts through the door, clink and a clunk goes the lock and the thick heavy steel door swings back. It is bright, "clean out & breakfast in ten", I have no idea what the prison guard means but I am about to walk out through that door and find it all out. Thanks again to all of you.

Love you Darra, Patrick & Alana. xoxoxo

Please feel free to join me on Twitter or Facebook.

@TWOsonTOOmany.

@17&Life3

All and any feedback greatly appreciated. 1 Luv.

Printed in Poland
by Amazon Fulfillment
Poland Sp. z o.o., Wrocław